MW01710430

Wesley L. Duewel

June 3, 1916 — March 5, 2016

All For Jesus

by
David E. Dick

Vice Chairman
Duewel Literature Trust, Inc.
617 Horton Street
Greenwood, Indiana 46142-4023

Printed by Spotlight-Strategies
Franklin, Indiana 46131

ISBN 978-1-880338-54-4

First Printing – 2016
10, 9, 8, 7, 6, 5, 4, 3, 2,

Acknowledgments

One Mission Society (OMS) and the Duewel Literature Trust (DLT) have compiled this collection of tributes to Dr. Wesley Duewel, with the assistance of Mr. **George** F. **Allen**, author and freelance consultant, and the professional publishing services of Mrs. Susan McCarty and Mr. James Bova at *Spotlight-Strategies* of Franklin, Indiana.

Previously, the editor began contacting various former OMS missionaries who knew and co-labored together with Dr. Duewel Therefore, we are deeply indebted to many others for the contents of this Memorial Book; especially the late Dr. Edward Erny, Rev. Robert Erny, Rev. Lowell Williamson, and of course, his faithful secretary, wife, and caregiver, Mrs. Hilda Duewel.

Sincere gratitude is expressed to all the contributors to this memorial booklet, none of which were aware when they submitted their tributes that they would end up forming the content of this book. Nevertheless, without their participation, this work would not have been possible. This collection of tributes serves as an interim account of Dr. Duewel's life and impact, until his autobiography is completed.

And to the Duewel family members for your personal remembrances, and Dr. Duewel's large circle of friends, who contributed kind words and remembrances, through the tributes contained herein, we are indebted. We trust this publication encourages everyone who reflects upon it to emulate the life, commitment, and example of Dr. Duewel, who lived his life, *"All for Jesus."*

A special thanks goes to Mrs. Hilda M. Duewel and Mrs. Celia E. Dick who painstakingly, read, reread, proofed, and re-proofed the manuscript. Any remaining mistakes, typos, or other form of errata remain the responsibility of the general editor.

Dr. Wesley Duewel's Life Verse[1]

"Enlarge the place of your tent,
stretch your tent curtains wide,
do not hold back;
lengthen your cords,
strengthen your stakes.
For you will spread out to the right and to the left;
your descendants will dispossess nations
and settle in their desolate cities." (Isaiah 54:2-3)

---

[1] While in college together, and before Wesley and Betty were married, this passage was discovered to be their common life verse. Later, before they shipped out for India, they discovered Mrs. Lettie Cowman, the 3rd president of OMS, also claimed this passage as her life verse. And upon arrival in India, they once again discovered this same passage was also the life verse of William Carey, commonly known as the Father of Modern Missions.

Preface

One of the most well-known and beloved leaders of OMS graduated to glory on Saturday, March 5, 2016. After giving his heart and soul to the cause of Christ around the world for the better part of 99 years, Dr. Wesley Duewel received his reward for faithfulness and fruitfulness, following a period of recurring hospitalizations. He suffered a massive stroke and after five hours of excellent medical care at a local hospital, he passed on to his eternal reward at 11:50 p.m. Although his earthly tabernacle expired, his eternal body received an everlasting robe of righteousness, as His Savior and Lord, Jesus Christ, welcomed him to the Throne of Grace with the words, '*Well done my good and faithful servant.*'

We express our deepest condolences to Mrs. Hilda Mae (Johnecheck) Duewel, his devoted secretary, wife, caregiver, and the entire Duewel family. He will be especially missed by Hilda, his son Dr. John Duewel, daughters Mrs. Christine (Duewel) Zahniser, and Mrs. Darlene (Duewel) Rueger as well as their children and grandchildren, and the entire extended worldwide OMS family. Wesley Duewel was ...

"a man of many peers, but few equals."

Rev. Louis and Mrs. Ida Duewel, Wesley's Parents

Foreword

"If ever there was a man who was sanctified, this man was." I was sitting at the kitchen table with Mrs. Hilda Duewel, whose husband, Dr. Wesley Duewel, had just passed away. She was describing him honestly after having worked closely with him over many years as his secretary, then in more recent years having become his wife. She was overwhelmingly grateful for the years God had given her with Dr. Duewel. While her deep sense of loss was palpable, her tremendous love, respect and appreciation for this God-adoring, Christ-loving, Spirit-filled man were abundantly evident.

In the following pages you will see all of this richly reinforced by many voices, from many perspectives. May you be encouraged and challenged by these testimonies from people who knew Dr. Wesley Duewel and were deeply impacted by his life and ministry. While my personal relationship with him was more recent and relatively short, I knew from my first visit with him that I was in the presence of a spiritual giant. I join the many others in these pages who give thanks to God for Dr. Wesley Duewel.

Dr. Duewel's response to all of this would be, *"All glory to Jesus!"* May our hearts echo this, and may we live in an abiding relationship with Jesus Christ, for as long as God gives us breath.

With great respect and much thanks,
Robert L. **Fetherlin**, President
One Mission Society, Greenwood, IN

Wesley and his parents

Table of Contents

The Wesley Duewel Family circa 1960

Introduction

Dr. Wesley Duewel is known for his passion for Christ, his family, and his many friends around the world. More than anything he is known for his deep abiding prayer passion for evangelism, revival, and missions. It is in keeping with this passion that OMS and DLT invite readers to enjoy the following collection of tributes, presented in the format of the actual Memorial Service, with the hope that the Spirit of Christ will be experienced in the hearts and lives of those who remember and reflect again on the life and impact of Dr. Wesley Duewel. We also ask the reader to prayerfully consider honoring the memory of Dr. Duewel by making a contribution to the Wesley Duewel Memorial Fund, extending and expanding his ministry passion, in India and through the DLT, further inspiring others to emulate living their lives as Dr. Duewel lived his: *All for Jesus*!

Memorial Fund #408169 Information

Giving to the memorial fund will continue Dr. Duewel's work in the ministries nearest and dearest to his heart, India and his book ministry. Thousands upon thousands of souls have been changed for eternity because of his intercession and inspirational publishing ministry. This memorial publication is for the express purpose of providing a continuing inspiration and reminder of his legacy to everyone who graciously remembers him through their contributions to the Wesley Duewel Memorial Fund. All memorial gifts should be sent to One Mission Society, PO Box 1648, Monument, CO 80132-1648. Thank you for making checks payable to OMS and designated to the Wesley Duewel Memorial Fund Project #408169 on the memo line.

Wesley three years and five months

Order of Worship

Prelude	*Make Me a Blessing* Mr. **Kenneth Platt**, Organist
Prayer	Rev. **Deborah Somerville**, Host Pastor *West Morris Free Methodist Church*
Hymn	*For All the Saints #546 (verses 1, 2, 6, 7)* Dr. **Mike E. Conkle**, Worship Leader, Former Senior Pastor, *West Morris Street Free Methodist Church*
Scripture	Isaiah 62:1-3, 6, 7; Isaiah 64:1-4 Dr. **David C. Long**, Former President *One Mission Society*
Hymn	*Crown Him with Many Crowns #234* (verses 1, 3, 4)
Video	**Lifetime of Service Award** (Video Tribute 2007) *OMS Communications*
Tributes	Dr. **Robert L. Fetherlin**, President *One Mission Society* Dr. **Mike E. Conkle**, Former Senior Pastor *West Morris Street Free Methodist Church* Dr. **John Wesley Duewel**, Son Mrs. Ruth **Christine Duewel** Zahniser, Daughter Mrs. Esther **Darlene Duewel** Rueger, Daughter
Hymn	*My Savior First of All* (verses 1, 2, 3, 4)

Message	Dr. **David E. Dick**, Vice President at Large *One Mission Society*
Prayer	Dr. **Robert L. Fetherlin**
Solo	*I Dreamed I Searched Heaven for You* Mr. **Jeff Bick**, Vocal Soloist Mrs. **Joyce Oden**, Accompanist
Poem	*'Tis Jesus! Heaven Has Begun!* Mr. **Jason M. Campbell** *OMS Communications*
Music	*It Is Well With My Soul* *All Ministers in Attendance*
Benediction	Dr. **David C. Long**
Recessional	*Hallelujah Chorus*

Scripture

An Amazingly New Identity

For Zion's sake I will not keep silent, for Jerusalem's sake I will not remain quiet, till her vindication shines out like the dawn, her salvation like a blazing torch. The nations will see your vindication, and all kings your glory; you will be called by a new name that the mouth of the LORD will bestow. You will be a crown of splendor in the LORD's hand, a royal diadem in the hand of your God. I have posted watchmen on your walls, Jerusalem; they will never be silent day or night. You who call on the LORD, give yourselves no rest, and give him no rest till he establishes Jerusalem and makes her the praise of the earth (Isaiah 62:1-3, 6, 7).

Our Incomprehensible – Unimaginable – Glorious God

Oh, that you would rend the heavens and come down, that the mountains would tremble before you! As when fire sets twigs ablaze and causes water to boil, come down to make your name known to your enemies and cause the nations to quake before you! For when you did awesome things that we did not expect, you came down, and the mountains trembled before you. Since ancient times no one has heard, no ear has perceived, no eye has seen any God besides you, who acts on behalf of those who wait for him (Isaiah 64:1-4).

Make Me a Blessing

Out in the highways and byways of life,
Many are weary and sad;
Carry the sunshine where darkness is rife,
Making the sorrowing glad.

Refrain:
Make me a blessing,
Make me a blessing,
Out of my life may Jesus shine;
Make me a blessing,
O Savior, I pray,
Make me a blessing to someone today.

Tell the sweet story of Christ and His love,
Tell of His power to forgive;
Others will trust Him if only you prove
True, every moment you live.

Give as ‘twas given to you in your need.
Love as the Master loved you;
Be to the helpless a helper indeed,
Unto your mission be true.

Ira B. Wilson, 1880–1950

Life Review

For All the Saints (verses 1. 2, 6, 7)

For all the saints who from their labors rest
Who Thee by faith before the world confessed,
Thy name, O Jesus, be forever blest.

Thou wast their rock, their fortress and their might;
Thou, Lord, their captain in the well-fought fight;
Thou, in the darkness drear, their one true light.

But lo! There breaks a yet more glorious day;
The saints triumphant rise in bright array;
The King of Glory passes on His way.

From earth's wide bounds, from ocean's farthest coast,
Thro' gates of pearl stream in the countless host,
Singing to Father, Son, and Holy Ghost.

(After stanza 7)
Alleluia! Alleluia! Amen.

William W. How, 1823–1897

Wesley Duewel Life Review

Remembering Dr. Wesley Duewel, Husband, Father, Friend, Missionary Pioneer, Executive, Statesman, Author, and Intercessor

Introduction:

Dr. Wesley Duewel was *'a man who may have had many peers, but seldom an equal.'* That's why when we realize that a spiritual giant, a living legend, has passed from our midst, our hearts and minds turn quickly to Psalm 116:15, *"Precious in the sight of the Lord is the death of His saints"* (KJV). The New International Version reads: *"Precious in the sight of the Lord is the death of his faithful servants."*

The Psalmist, King David, always thought of God as very intimately involved in the lives of His people. David comforted himself with this reality in the depth of his distress and danger; many times over his experience confirmed it. As David writes this Psalm, he comforts others with this truth and reality. Whoever might be in danger, distress, or discouragement, may take heart and be encouraged. Nothing occurs in the life of a child of God that the Lord is not intimately aware of, and concerned for, and that is especially so for those who have lost a loved one in the Lord. May you be consoled and comforted with this reality. It seems that indeed God extended Dr. Duewel's life for nearly a century so that in and through him, God could accomplish the most and highest good possible.

Anyone who met and knew Dr. Duewel were different as a result. The people we meet and get to know personally become part of us. Most who read his books were likewise positively impacted. Dr. Duewel has become part of each one who knew him and each one who read his books. His life will continue to speak meaningful things to those he touched as long as they live.

However, because this life review does not comply with his last wishes at his funeral to minimize him and maximize Jesus, much of what was compiled and given to me from others has been composed into the life review that follows.[1]

One of Dr. Duewel's last writing projects was his autobiography. He compiled seven, thick, three-ring binders, each representing many years of his life and ministry. He was having trouble trying to consolidate and synthesize the rich and rewarding life that God had given to him. He was fearful that he would shortchange God. If he couldn't do it, how can I hope to do so in this brief review? My apologies for summarizing his life in five, very brief, categories.

Parents Louis and Ida with newborn Wesley

The Son and Little Minister

Wesley Duewel was born on June 3, 1916 in St. Charles, Missouri, to Louis J. and Ida (Luelf) Duewel. Being born into a pastor's family, he was *"raised in the fear and admonition of the Lord"* with consistent discipline, as well as constant assurance of their love.

His father was a very godly, sweet-spirited gentleman who supported his family through serving as an evangelist, Methodist pastor, Bible teacher

---

[1] The author is especially indebted to the late Dr. Edward Erny for many of the details that follow.

and preacher, Bible college president, radio speaker, and a leading light in the Fire Baptized Holiness Church (now Bible Holiness Church). Wesley recounted that on the day and moment of entering their family home for his father's memorial service, he heard his father's final message being broadcast over the radio.

Parents Louis and Ida with young Wesley

His mother was a godly and devout woman who was bedridden for many years, and painfully sensitive to light and noise. Nevertheless, and perhaps because of her frail condition, she was well known for her intercessory prayer ministry, continuously praying for members of their congregation, her husband's ministry, others in their community and around the world, because missions was a great burden on her heart. On one occasion she had saved up nearly $1,000 for the cause of missions. That was no small sum of money in those days, and certainly went a lot farther than today. On this occasion she was ill with appendicitis. She prayed, *"Oh Lord, I don't want to give all this money to a hospital and doctors. If you will just heal me, I will send this money to OMS for the China ministry."* She was healed instantly and followed through on her promise to God.

Life Review

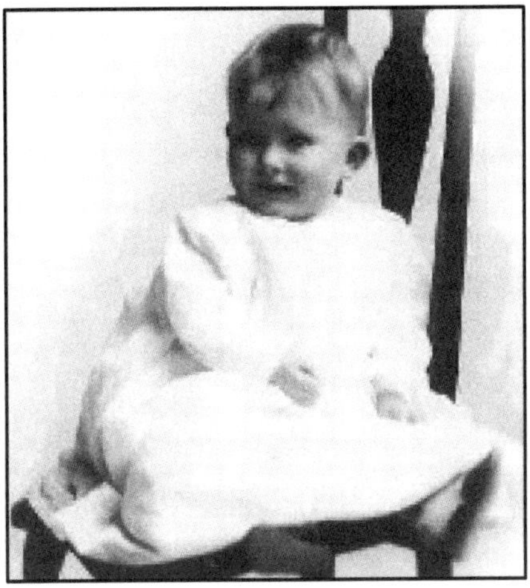

Young Wesley

From his earliest childhood, Wesley was endowed with prodigious interest in spiritual matters. Wesley's personal childhood conversion was something that he never tired of retelling, no doubt because of his mother's sustaining influence on his life. He was a small child of two or three years of age, and while his mother was praying for him prior to his being tucked into bed, he exclaimed: *"O Mommy, don't stop praying. It's doing me lots of good."* The next thing his mother knew, Wesley had jumped off the bed onto the floor, saying, *"O Mommy, I'm so happy! Jesus just came into my heart, and I can't stop jumping!"*

As a boy of no more than five years of age, Wesley was playing in his sandbox in the parsonage yard beside his father's church in Nashville, Illinois, making tracks in the sand for his little toy cars, when suddenly the Lord spoke to him. Startled, he jumped up and listened, and then ran into the house exclaiming, *"O Mama, Jesus has just told me that when I get big He wants me to go to India to tell people about Him. Mama, I want you to go along with me."* As he testified over and over, she did, through her continuous prevailing prayer, until she preceded him into heaven in 1962.

Wesley playing outside

Wesley recounted he does not remember actually hearing or seeing Jesus in a vision when Jesus spoke to him. He never recalled there was any special missionary services in the weeks preceding this experience. But from that point on in his life, he was certain that God wanted him to be a missionary to India, and he never lost the wonder of that clear call from his youth. He was so intent on spiritual matters as a young person that he earned the nick name, *"The Little Minister."*

This clear sense of God's guidance and direction, as well as new multifaceted dimensions of that very personal call kept him and sustained him throughout his undergraduate, post-graduate, executive leadership days, and post-presidency period of a very productive and fruitful life.

The Scholar and Husband

If 'time travel' were a reality, and we went back to visit the Duewel family home, we would see on their living room table, many turn of the century holiness magazines featuring articles by famous holiness preachers like Henry Clay Morrison, 'Uncle Buddy Robinson,' A.M. Hillis, and Oswald Chambers. Alongside these, one issue, arranged with care, was *"God's Revivalist,"* published by God's Bible School (GBS). So, it was only logical, when Wesley graduated from high school in Nebraska, he would apply and enroll at GBS.

Life Review

Wesley learned about OMS while attending camp meetings as a child, reading OMS literature, and hearing OMS speakers. While attending GBS, consistent with his sense of boyhood calling, Wesley had inquired twice, asking about the possibility of serving in India, and if OMS would ever consider entering India. At that time, OMS had no active ministry in India nor any indication that they would open India as an OMS field of service. OMS representatives seemed to discount his inquiry, explaining that OMS had too much to do in Japan, Korea, and China. Wesley was counseled not to *"boss"* God. Wesley explained that he *"was not bossing God, God was bossing him!"* In fact, *'Great War'* clouds were gathering on the horizon and threatening OMS fields in Japan, Korea, and China. Although the mission had indeed been giving serious thought about opening India, since it was still a relatively tranquil British colony, Wesley was told: *"OMS presently has no work in India, but the board is considering it. You pray about it and we'll pray also."*

Wesley met Elizabeth Dolly Raisch (better known as Betty), also a student at GBS. She was extremely attractive, and an outstanding scholar. School policies strictly regimented social relationships among students of opposite genders on campus. But circumstances developed that facilitated a courtship. Betty was employed in the college library and Wesley worked as an assistant professor, which classified them both as staff members. Therefore, they were not subject to the same social restrictions. Although their budding romance was obvious to the alert observer, no one felt constrained to obstruct or hinder the relationship between these two young people who so obviously loved one another and the Lord, and they were planning to serve Him as missionaries in India. On their first date, they made a wonderful discovery. God had given them both the same life verse from Isaiah 54:2-3a: *"Enlarge the place of your tent; stretch your tent curtains wide, do not hold back;*

lengthen your cords, strengthen your stakes. For you will spread out to the right and to the left."

Wesley prayed daily for two years. He retreated into the library after hours and knelt by a world globe, lit inside by a dim bulb. He prayed for six points: 1) Send a society to India with the same doctrines and priorities as OMS; 2) Place the burden for India on the heart of that society's leader; 3) Call others so the society could begin with a small team; 4) Prepare Indian coworkers who were free to serve alongside these new team members, without taking them from another mission group or ministry; 5) Provide a large monetary gift so this team could launch the new work, and 6) Place a burden on the heart of a group of people to pray for that society.

In May 1938 Wesley received his A.B. degree, and in 1939 his Th.B. degree, the same year in which Betty also received her A.B. degree from GBS. Wesley graduated as valedictorian, Betty as class salutatorian, both with highest (Summa Cum Laude) honors. A month later on June 29, 1939, they were married in Cincinnati, and then returned to his parent's home in Missouri. Sometime later, after attending a local camp meeting, they returned home to discover a cablegram from Seoul, Korea on his father's front porch. Dr. Eugene Erny had written to announce the OMS Board voted unanimously to enter India. Wesley and Betty's prayers had been answered. The cablegram went on to encourage: *"If interested, apply at once."* They did so, but OMS required one year of active pastoral ministry, so they served in a pastorate in Barnsdall, Oklahoma for one year.

Betty and Wesley were among the first small group of seven missionaries who sailed for India to pioneer the OMS work. They were bid farewell at the home of Mrs. Lettie B. Cowman in Los Angeles, on December 30,

Wesley and Betty Duewel - 1940

1940. In her challenge to them Mrs. Cowman gave them the same life verse they had claimed together at GBS. They were told it had been Charles Cowman's life verse and, upon arrival in India, discovered it had been William Carey's life verse as well! For 68 years Betty and Wesley served side by side, one year in the Oklahoma pastorate, 25 years in India, and then for 42 years in Greenwood, at the world headquarters of OMS. During those 25 years in Allahabad, India, God blessed Betty and Wesley with three children, John Wesley (1944), Ruth Christine (1946), and Esther Darlene (1956). The children's recollections of their father's personal life are recorded in the family tribute section.

The Missionary Pioneer and Professor

As an OMS missionary, Dr. Duewel was a brilliant man, shining with peculiar luster. He was truly giving his all for God. As a young man he roamed the dirty, dusty, trails of rural India speaking to whomever would gather as an audience. God fulfilled the desire of his heart by giving him the joy of pioneering the OMS work located initially in Allahabad, North India. He served as seminary professor and principal of Allahabad Bible Seminary. He led the North India Christian Literature Society, as well as the Bible Society of India, and helped spearhead the founding of the Evangelical Fellowship of India (EFI). He also served on the boards of various organizations within India. When Dr. Eugene Erny was called to succeed Mrs. Lettie B. Cowman as OMS President, Wesley was chosen to carry on and serve as the OMS India Field Director. In 2009, the EFI gave him the *"Lifetime Service Award in recognition of his servant leadership exemplified in the Body of Christ and faithful contribution to the Church and Mission in India."*

His burden for India throughout those years in India was to see a harvest for Jesus! He worked hard to establish a Spirit-filled praying national church. He led special revival meetings semi-annually for seminary students. He tried earnestly to instill within them daily habits of prevailing prayer. He led half days of prayer, days of prayer, nights of prayer, times of prayer and fasting, conferences on prayer, workshops on prayer, and seminars on prayer.

For 25 years Wesley carried a special burden for a Spirit-filled, praying church in India. But after trying their very best by word and deed, the OMS India field could show very little fruit. He helped establish three formal Bible seminaries, one for each major geographical and linguistic region, in the north, central, and south. He helped establish the first 25 formally incorporated local congregations of today's formally registered and recognized Evangelical Church of India. These local congregations represented about 1,500 formally baptized members. Every ministry activity was earmarked with faithfulness in the harvest and earnest prayer.

Nevertheless, discouragement was not far away. Working among Hindus and Muslims was never easy. But seeds sown in tears were going to produce fruit in the future. *"Those who sow with tears will reap with songs of joy. Those who go out weeping, carrying seed to sow, will return with songs of joy, carrying sheaves with them"* (Psalm 126:5-6).

The Missionary President and Statesman

Wesley and Betty Duewel at Headquarters

Returning for an OMS Board meeting in 1964, somewhere over the Pacific, between Honolulu and Los Angeles, Wesley prayed again: *"Oh Lord, give us 1,000 people who will commit themselves to pray for 15 minutes a day for at least one year, specifically for our OMS India work."* God honored that prayer with 1,500 people from 32 nations who prayed over the next twelve months. It was a 'spiritual jump start' which broke down barriers and opened the way for the Gospel to advance like never before.

The growth and development of the Evangelical Church of India (ECI) was slow, starting with one church every year for the first 25 years, then increasing to one church every month over the next 25 years, then one church every week over the next ten years, then three churches every week over the next ten years. Today the ECI consists of over 16,896 churches, a membership of over 750,000 and growing at the rate of approximately 4½ churches weekly. The ECI Centennial goal is for establishing 100,000 churches with 10 million members. What made the difference? We firmly believe it was that breakthrough prayer effort, along with the deeply embedded prayer habit sown deep within the ECI that shaped those foundational years and continues to manifest itself in ECI throughout India.

After 25 years of full-time field ministry, 17 years in the executive leadership of OMS, and another 21 years as President Emeritus and Founder of Duewel Literature Trust (DLT), as the old saying goes, "*You can take the missionary out the field, but you can never take the field out of the missionary*." This held true for Wesley. When the Lord called him to take up the mantle of the presidency of OMS in 1969, his specific call to India became his more fully-rounded worldwide call for a total of 75 years in ministry.

While Dr. Duewel served as President and CEO, he carried a heavy burden for personnel and strategic outreach. He trusted his Vice Presidents to carry on the functions of administration. He cast vision, and inspired others with his Spirit-filled oratory and proclamation, and he contributed much to the operational outreach of OMS traditional three-fold focus, evangelism, church planting, and theological education.

I can still remember the passion and urgency with which Dr. Duewel preached on Ezekiel 33 at one of the earliest annual OMS annual conventions that my wife and I attended.

God has made you a watchman!

> *The word of the LORD came to me: "Son of man, speak to your people and say to them: 'When I bring the sword against a land, and the people of the land choose one of their men and make him their watchman, and he sees the sword coming against the land and blows the trumpet to warn the people, then if anyone hears the trumpet but does not heed the warning and the sword comes*

> *and takes their life, their blood will be on their own head. Since they heard the sound of the trumpet but did not heed the warning, their blood will be on their own head. If they had heeded the warning, they would have saved themselves. But if the watchman sees the sword coming and does not blow the trumpet to warn the people and the sword comes and takes someone's life, that person's life will be taken because of their sin, but I will hold the watchman accountable for their blood.'*
>
> *"Son of man, I have made you a watchman for the people of Israel; so hear the word I speak and give them warning from me. When I say to the wicked, 'You wicked person, you will surely die,' and you do not speak out to dissuade them from their ways, that wicked person will die for their sin, and I will hold you accountable for their blood. But if you do warn the wicked person to turn from their ways and they do not do so, they will die for their sin, though you yourself will be saved* (Ezekiel 33:1-9).

He declared, if we, the Church, do not act responsibly, the blood of the lost will be on our hands. But if we, the Church, do act responsibly, and the lost ignore, or reject, the Good News of salvation available in Jesus Christ, then their blood will remain on their hands, but we, the Church, will not be held accountable.

I left that annual conference with a new sense of responsibility to be involved in the Great Commission, sharing the Good News of salvation in Jesus Christ with those who had never heard before. I trace my own personal call and commitment to serve with OMS in cross-cultural missions to that particular convention and that particular message from the Lord through His messenger.

When I was accepted into the mission, Dr. Duewel had formally cast the vision for the '*Decade of Harvest*.' The goals were far greater than anything ever attempted to date. Every field was called to pray, plan, and report how they would contribute to the overall goals of the mission. At the conclusion of that particular decade, OMS reported one of the greatest harvests that the mission had ever seen. The OMS outreach footprint increased into four new countries, with 100 new evangelism and church planting teams who reported 160,000 first-time decisions for Christ, who were incorporated into 600 new congregations over that ten-year period. Never before in the history of OMS had such six-digit numbers in decisions and three-digit numbers in new churches been reported over a ten-year period. Dr. Duewel proved the merit of his selection to the presidency of OMS through the continuation of faith-based vision casting supported with intercessory prayer and strategic outreach which has characterized OMS spiritual DNA since its founding.

The Author and Intercessor

When he stepped down from the presidency of OMS one of the International Board members suggested, "*Perhaps God wants you to write some*." He hadn't written formally since his days in India when he was writing and editing the ***Revival*** magazine, published in 12 languages. God led him into another chapter of his life during which he wrote ten books on the Holy Spirit, prayer, revival, and the deeper life. As a writer and author, he left monuments of his piety, purity, and power, which have been a blessing to many millions of people worldwide, and doubtless will be a blessing for many ages to come. Dr. Duewel, with the faithful assistance of Hilda, has managed to publish and distribute his ten major books in 58 languages, with a world-wide circulation of 2.5 million copies. Moreover, the financial investment making this possible has amounted to more than one million dollars, provided through the DLT which has been shouldered by Wesley and Hilda since the trust's inception, devoid of any personal remuneration. When asked about such a major accomplishment, he would humbly reply, *"To God be all the glory*!"

He continued to minister through his writing and publication ministry under the auspices of the DLT. He left a virtual treasure trove of poetry and poems never published, but always included copies in his routine correspondence and annual letters. These were always selected for the purpose at hand. How he managed to compose such depth and quality in the context of the unpaved, dusty, dirty roads of rural India, and produce draft after draft of lectures, devotionals, poems and poetry, never ceased to amaze me, and all those who realized what a non-stop energized person he must have been during his prime.

He continued to pray for the literature ministry on a regular basis. If you stopped by his office throughout the week in the early morning, you'd find him faithfully reading the Word. He had a tremendous love for God's Word and read it daily since childhood. He read the entire Bible 209 times and the New Testament 354 times. He continued to carry a constant burden for the un-evangelized millions of the world, his constant emphasis upon prayer was the key to harvest and revival.

As an individual, few have appeared with less defect, and few have reached similar glowing heights of sanctification, and not been arrogant doing so. The primary and prominent feature of his life was his devotion to the Word of God and prayer. Like many who have gone before him, and from whom he no doubt learned, his underlying message was: *"When I pray and meditate the most, I accomplish the most*." This was the guiding principle of his actions, public and private. He was always diligent, anxious to do the right thing, be humble, demonstrate patience, and serve zealously, always motivated with love for God, his adored Redeemer and Friend, and his fellow man.

Over a period of time, when it became increasingly evident the Lord could take him at any moment, I began to think of what could be said about this great, but humble man since I was his backup as speaker for his memorial service. Regrettably, his first choice, Rev. Dr. Donald Riggs, one of the longest tenured Senior Pastors of the West Morris Street Free Methodist Church, long the home church of Dr. Duewel, preceded him to glory. As I thought of the beautiful, figurative language of John Bunyan in his classical *Pilgrim's Progress*, I imagined Dr. Duewel expressing himself in similar fashion:

> *I might date these final words from the land of Beulah, of which for some weeks I have entertained being a happy inhabitant. The celestial city is in full view. Its glories beam upon me. Its breezes cool me. Its fragrance wafted over me. Its music strikes my ears. And its spirit is breathed into my heart. Nothing separates me from it but the river of death, which now appears but as an insignificant rill that may be crossed at a single step, whenever God shall give permission. The Sun of righteousness has been gradually drawing near and nearer, appearing larger and brighter as He approached, and now fills the whole hemisphere, pouring forth a flood of glory, in which I seem to float like an insect in the beams of the sun, exulting, yet almost trembling, while I gaze upon His excessive brilliance, and wondering, with unutterable wonder, why God should willingly shine with such wondrous glory upon such a lowly, unworthy, man as me.* John Bunyan, *Pilgrim's Progress*

Life Review

The Old Testament Prophet Isaiah comforts us with these words: *"Your sun will never set again, and your moon will wane no more; the Lord will be your everlasting light, and your days of sorrow will end"* (Isaiah 60:20).

Yet another spiritual leader looked upon his own graduation to glory in this manner: *"O what a blessed day that will be when I shall . . . stand on the shore and look back on the raging seas I have safely passed; when I shall review my pains and sorrows, my fears and tears, and possess the glory which was the end of all!"*[2]

Another leader had instructed that a plaque be inscribed and laid across his coffin so that all those who passed by at his viewing might yet be addressed.[3]

"I have fought the good fight, I have finished the race, I have kept the faith. Now there is in store for me the crown of righteousness, which the Lord, the righteous Judge, will award to me on that day—and not only to me, but also to all who have longed for his appearing" (2 Timothy 4:7-8).

John Wesley, the 18th century Anglican pastor who founded the Methodist movement, for whom Dr. Duewel was likely named, repeated these final words:

I'll praise my maker while I've breath,
And when my voice is lost in death,
Praise shall employ my nobler powers:
My days of praise shall ne'er be past,
While life, and thought, and being last,
Or immortality endures!

---

[2] Richard Baxter, a 17th century English Puritan church leader

[3] Edward Payson's death, a 19th century American Congregational preacher

Life Review

To Father, Son and Holy Ghost
Who sweetly all agree, -
The best of all is,
God is with us.

In closing, although Wesley Duewel is no longer with us, his life lives on through his wife, Hilda; his children, John, Christine, and Darlene; and your children, and your children's children. Wesley Duewel will always be a part of the lives of those whom he loved and touched. His loss to the family is also a great loss to OMS and to the world.

Hilda, John, Christine, and Darlene, imagine Wesley's voice as you read these closing lines from his personal testimony.

> Several years ago God gave me the promise of Psalm 91:16: "*With long life will I satisfy him and show him my salvation*." God has wonderfully fulfilled that promise for me, and now I am in the presence of the One who loved me and gave Himself for me. In recent years, I have closed most of my correspondence with my constant heart-cry, "*All for Jesus*."

Yes, He answers prayer today, in the same old fashioned way.
He will grant us our petitions, if we truly pray!

In the words of the well-known hymn of James Montgomery in 1819:

Servant of God, well done! Rest from thy loved employ;
The battle fought, the victory won, Earth thy master's joy.

Life Review

Soldier of Christ, well done! Praise be thy new employ;
And while eternal ages run, Rest in thy Savior's joy.

With my deepest love and sincere condolences,
David E. **Dick,** VP At Large
One Mission Society, Greenwood, IN

The righteous are held in everlasting remembrance.

Crown Him with Many Crowns (verses 1, 2, 4)

Crown Him with many crowns,
The Lamb upon His throne;
Hark! How the heavenly anthem drowns
All music but its own!
Awake, my soul, and sing
Of Him who died for thee,
And hail Him as thy matchless King
Through all eternity.

Crown Him the Son of God
Before the worlds began,
And ye, who tread where He hath trod,
Crown Him the Son of man;
Who every grief hath known
That wrings the human breast,
And takes and bears them for His own,
That all in Him may rest.

Crown Him the Lord of love!
Behold His hands and side,
Rich wounds, yet visible above,
In beauty glorified:
All hail, Redeemer, hail!
For Thou hast died for me:
Thy praise shall never, never fail
Throughout eternity.

Matthew Bridges, 1800–1894, and Godfrey Thring, 1823–1903

Family Tributes

Tribute to Dad: Celebrating a Long Life, Well Lived

Introduction and Rationale

These comments cover the same themes in the presentation I made during the funeral service tribute to my dad, Wesley Luelf Duewel. The ceremony cum celebration of a life of service was held on March 15, 2016, at the West Morris Street Free Methodist Church in Indianapolis, Indiana. Dad attended and found a home in this particular church for about five decades. Until recently he also taught a weekly senior Sunday school class there.

I organized my oral tribute to Dad, along with this lengthier and elaborated written version, in themes and vignettes. These tribute reminiscences are based on experiences and interactions with Dad, as his son, accompanied by observations and insights gleaned from some of my dad's stories. My personal direct interactions with Mom and Dad were frequent and regular, continuing up to two months before my dad's passing. They typically centered on annual visits that my wife, Retno and I, and our two children, Santi and David, would make to Greenwood during the last 40 years.

Sometimes these visits were long drives, often through snow, from Cornell University in Ithaca, New York, around Christmas. More frequently and during the last 20 years they've centered on annual year-end 'pilgrimage' trips from Indonesia where I have lived and worked for the last 30 years.

In recent years, following Mom's passing and Dad's marriage to Hilda, I have been able to make two trips a year to Greenwood, but of shorter duration. In making these trips, especially when my children were young and growing up, Retno and I always took the view that they should share space every year with their grandparents, in addition to spending time in the U.S.

Early Days with Mom, and Hilda's Evolving Roles

My dad was an only child, raised in small towns in Illinois, Kansas and Missouri, where his father pastored churches of the Fire Baptized Holiness Church, typically consisting of German American Methodists. My mom, by contrast, was one of eight children (and the oldest daughter) growing up on a farm with a sawmill near Cincinnati, Ohio. Weekend visits to that farm during 1948–1952 period, when my dad pursued doctoral studies and I was starting school, were one of the highlights of my childhood.

What my mom and dad had in common was essentially 100% German ancestry (in the case of my dad, German Methodist immigrants who arrived from the Prussian area of North Germany some 160+ years ago in 1852). Dad was not out to maintain a pure German–American lineage and find a lifetime Fraulein. Rather, their German connection was by chance. They met at God's Bible School, discovered they shared the same life verse, with Mom graduating as Salutatorian of her class one year after Dad who graduated Valedictorian (Mom was eight days short of being one year older than Dad). Soon after graduation they married, just prior to the outbreak of World War II, with Mom knowing their life would be adventurous and would most likely involve moving to India, given my dad's calling. On December 31, 1940, they set out for India with OMS via an American passenger ocean liner, to help open up a new mission field for OMS. They initially stayed in India for eight years, through the war years and extending until 1948, eventually returning to the U.S. 24 years later in 1964 following several terms of service.

Hilda, from northern Michigan, of Czech ancestry, has served loyally and faithfully as Dad's secretary, organizer, member of the DLT, and been a personal friend of mine since the mid–1960s. She has been Dad's loving wife and caretaker for the last seven years, in addition to continuing office duties. During this time she has age-proofed the house, and devoted endless amounts of care, attention and energy, enabling Dad to live out his life at home. For this sharing of his life, my siblings and I are very grateful. Until the last six months of his life, when Dad no longer went to his office regularly, Hilda alternated between being a wife at home, and Dad's secretary and office manager during his less regular time spent at the Research and Writing Center on the OMS campus. Also, deep appreciation goes to the OMS for allowing my dad to maintain his office until the end of his life.

Scholarly Heritage, Teacher: Lover of Books and Learning

Dad, following in the tradition of his father, Rev. Louis J. Duewel, was a scholar and lover of books on multiple themes and topics, as evidenced by his office library. My grandfather, in addition to serving as a minister, was also principal of a high school and Bible college in Kansas. I still have a copy of the booklet my grandfather researched and produced in 1953, filled with brief descriptions and photographs of multiple families in the Duewel post migration lineage, titled, *"One Hundred Years of Duewel History"* (1852-1952) in the U.S. While my dad often talked of his mom, I really liked my grandfather, who always had a friendly, earthy demeanor. I had the fortune to spend several days with him in Missouri on two occasions, after my grandmother passed. This included a brief visit at the end of the summer in 1962 when I was transitioning from high school in

India (and from three months of highway bridge construction in Hesston, Kansas) to college in Greenville, Illinois.

Dad did his Master's Degree in Education (M. Ed.) at the University of Cincinnati and, as I recall, shared a class with Oscar Robertson, of NBA Cincinnati Royals fame. He followed this by doing a Doctorate in Education (D. Ed.) that he completed in 1952. His doctoral dissertation, as I recall, focused on designing a seminary theological curriculum for a country that was multi–ethnic, multi–religion and multi–cultural, in this case, India. Thus, he had thought very carefully about the future direction of the Allahabad Bible Seminary where he served as Principal and teacher for many years.

Dad always kept a *World Book* encyclopedia at our house in India, and had a huge eclectic library of books on multiple topics, including volumes on India, its history, culture and religions. He also had many books on science, the universe and cosmology. I also recall that he had Rachel Carson's seminal environmental expose, '*The Silent Spring*', long before it was fashionable. As a child and later teenager in India–and later as an adult, in Dad's OMS office as well as the Horton Street home, following construction of an extension to the house, in part to accommodate books not kept in his office library—it was an adventure to explore his books.

One of the courses that Dad taught at the Allahabad Bible Seminary, in addition to such things as Hermeneutics, was Comparative Cosmology. In this course he compared Hindu, Islam, Sikh, Buddhist, Jewish, and Confucian (among others) concepts of meaning, causality, morality, ethics, views of history, eschatology, heaven, etc. He felt that the ministerial candidates, in order to be effective, should understand the diverse religious and cultural contexts of India. I used to play volleyball in the afternoons with seminary students who said Dad's course on

'*Comparative Cosmology*' was the toughest they took, but also the one from which they learned the most. I also recall that on several of my three-month winter vacations in Allahabad, Dad used to pay me small pittances to help him file thousands of his articles and clippings.

Dad spent several years studying Hindi and Urdu (the two major languages of North Central India), including their scripts (Arabic for Urdu; Devanagri–Sanskrit based for Hindi). He was so proficient linguistically that he served on the Hindi–Urdu language examining board (one of five examiners, including one other foreigner, Caldwell Smith, who was the Director) of the Indian Language Institute in Allahabad. This is where missionaries (and others) from all over India would attend for several years to study Indian languages and, in particular, Hindi and Urdu. I heard from Hilda that during a recent short stint in the nearby hospital, Dad would break into Hindi when talking to Indian doctors, who were impressed by his recall and memory.

Dad always encouraged me in my never–ending Ph.D. studies, and was relieved when I finally got around to completing my dissertation at Cornell University, in the field of Development Sociology of the Department of Rural Sociology. He also was interested in the studies of some of his grandchildren. In the case of our daughter, he followed her Master's Honor's thesis at the University of Edinburgh in Scotland in International Relations, and took time to look at her thesis, proposing a permanent UN peace keeping force. He and Mom had great fun and took pride in attending and participating in the events linked to our daughter Santi's graduation from Yale University in 2000, even though Mom was 85 and Dad was 84 at the time. Four years later, they were also proud to attend our son's combined M.A. and M.Sc. graduation at Indiana University. He would always say the Duewels followed a German tradition of engaging in rigorous scholarly pursuits.

A final comment relevant to this fairly long theme concerns an incident I recall from my high school years when I was on my annual three–month winter vacation at the big seminary complex in Allahabad. Late in the afternoon one day, I was walking near the swinging iron-entrance gate to the seminary compound where I encountered an elderly, fairly tall and white haired gentleman, with flowing white beard and a walking stick. He inquired about Dr. Duewel, who, he said, he had heard was a holy man and scholar teaching here. I indicated I was his son and escorted him to meet Dad at the house. Dad and the gentleman engaged in long intensive conversations, interspersed with dinner at the house. He and Dad talked well into the late hours of the night on Hindu philosophy, Christianity, pilgrimages to sacred sites in the mountains including Tibet. I learned the next day from Dad that the man was a retired professor from a prestigious Indian university with a Ph.D. from Oxford (or Cambridge) University in England. He had ventured on to the fourth and last Hindu 'Sunna Yasi' phase of a man's life based on Hindu concepts and, after leaving his family, had wandered and trekked to many sacred or holy pilgrimage sites in the Himalayas as far as Tibet. Somehow he had gotten Dad's name, and Dad took the time and enjoyed the challenge of engaging him in deep conversation for long hours about their differing experiences with and concepts of life. I am sure that Dad would have prayed with him before his departure.

Concern for Others: No Stranger to Danger

Communal conflict in northern India was rife during the late colonial period. Probably during 1947, when the partition and upcoming Independence of India was accompanied by millions of displaced Muslims and Hindus crossing borders, resulted in hundreds of thousands dying. At that time, Dad took a 24–hour train trip from Allahabad to Dehru Dun located at the edge of the foothills of the Himalayas, before taking the bus the 16 mile, steeply rising and winding, ride up 2,000 meters altitude to Mussoorie. The purpose in crossing conflict areas was to hand carry money for the missionaries residing there. At one junction station the train stopped for several hours in the middle of the night, sensing the presence of danger Dad was led to pray. His train was one of the first to be able to get through to the mountains safely.

Similarly, in 1947, in the midst of Indian partition when communal strife and urban riots were endemic, and mass killings were occurring in particular near to the border crossing points between India (Punjab) and what was then West Pakistan, and also between India (West Bengal) and what was then East Pakistan — now Bangladesh — on the east border. At this time Dad had traveled by train to the eastern city of Calcutta near the border, where riots were occurring. He was endeavoring to meet a new missionary family who were waiting on an ocean liner stranded in the harbor, until the conditions would improve. For several days Dad went down to the harbor, to no avail, and twice got caught up in the midst of rioters.

On one of these riot occasions, as a mob came running down the street, Dad managed to escape by jumping into a doorway where foreign troops were barracked. On another occasion, when mobs were running down the street, he managed to get picked up by two U.S. marines in an open–topped Willys jeep and jumped into the back. The two marines raced and forced their way into a park area where a foreign woman had been stripped naked and was being beaten. They grabbed the woman, dumped her in the back of the jeep with Dad, and raced to a hospital where she was transferred. Dad was warned by the marines to be careful on the streets. Eventually, after the rioting was brought under control,

Dad was able to meet the missionary family and return by train safely to Allahabad.

On February 3, 1954, a day after my tenth birthday, Dad took me with him to join and follow the procession of throngs (millions) of pilgrims on the peak day of the once in 12-year Kumbh Mela festival in Allahabad. The month-long festival was centered on the sacred Sangam confluence of the Ganges (Ganga) and Jumuna rivers with four – five million people attending during the peak full moon bathing day (Mauni Amadasya). At that time it was reputed to be the largest religious gathering that had been staged in the world, with millions of pilgrims attempting to bathe at and near the Sangam confluence on the peak day.

On that day, up to 3,000 people were trampled to death in a disaster broadcast world-wide. While we were in the midst of throngs of people during the height of the procession, and I was being pressed and cramped from all sides, I began to feel claustrophobic and expressed my concerns to Dad. He then forced his way up and climbed onto a bamboo police tower platform, followed by me, where we waited for several hours until the throngs of pilgrims in the procession thinned. We thereby avoided a stampede of a large group of sadhus, waving their sacred lance swords, trying to cross the procession, not far from the tower where an estimated 500 persons were trampled to death.

Love and Commitment to India (and Other Countries and Cultures)

Dad had a love for India that went far beyond Christian evangelism and his teaching of missions. Since the early 1940s he had an historical appreciation of the trajectory of India's history, and was an early supporter of its generally peaceful campaign for Independence. He would often dress in an Indian outfit when preaching at church.

Allahabad was then the center of India's Congress Party, and the location of the Nehru family residence that was down the road from the seminary. (The Nehrus moved from Allahabad to New Delhi, the capital of India, when India became independent during 1947.) When Jawaharlal Nehru, India's first prime minister, was in political detention by the British government in Allahabad, during the late colonial era, one of Dad's Presbyterian missionary friends, who knew Nehru, used to pass him books to read.

Dad and I have multiple pictures we took of Nehru close up, including a picture of Nehru riding on a horse in the hill station of Mussoorie in the Himalayan mountains. I also have a picture taken around 1959 or 1960 in which all the participants, of a special six-week cultural/historical introductory course at Allahabad University, posed with Prime Minister Nehru at the closing ceremony. Dad always had a good opinion of and respect for the succession of Indian Prime Ministers, including Indira Gandhi.

When I was younger, I would ride on the back of Dad's motorcycle when heading into the Civil Lines downtown section of Allahabad. I recall that Dad would always salute the traffic policemen at the traffic roundabouts in the middle of intersections, and say 'Jai-Hind' (Victory to India). I have used that phrase throughout my life when meeting Indians. A few weeks before Dad's passing, I received an e-mail from my son, David, as he was preparing to fly to India to participate in the wedding ceremony of one of his friends from New York City. He asked for some useful Indian phrases, and the first term I gave him was 'Jai-Hind.' David used it in all of his greetings, including when he met the father of the groom, who was a senior Indian Air Force Officer. The groom's father was quite surprised and intrigued, and asked David where he had picked up the 'Jai–Hind' term. Of course this led to a short narration about me, my birth and upbringing in Allahabad and schooling in the mountains. Dad's legacy continues.

In his post-India years, in addition to strongly supporting the national church in India, Dad always had a deep appreciation for the countries, peoples, church leaders and others that he visited, including an appreciation for their histories and cultural heritages. I know this is not unique to him as many missionaries have this cultural empathy and appreciation of other societies. In his office at OMS, and at home, there are numerous mementos and cultural artifacts, some of them gifts that have pride of place on his bookcase shelves, tables and walls.

Historical Justice and Fairness: 1965 Selma Civil Rights March

An aspect of Dad's character that is also linked to his respect for the cultures and traditions of people from other countries and societies was his sense of historical justice and fair play. This is evidenced by his great respect for Abraham Lincoln and his view on civil rights. During March of 1965, when I was a junior at Greenville College, an infamous and historical incident occurred on the Edumund Pettras Bridge in Selma, Alabama, when civil rights marchers were beaten up by police as they endeavored to march cross the bridge. After a brief follow–up crossing of the bridge by religious leaders a day or so later, plans were made for a major mobilization of marchers from all over the country to cross the bridge a week to ten days later, to be followed by a march to the state capital of Montgomery by a smaller group of civil rights marchers.

At Greenville College, where I was then Student Body Vice President, I had helped to organize two carloads of eight people (including four in my small sunroof VW) to travel to Selma to participate in the march. Unfortunately, the Greenville College administration at that time, including the College president (who was a non–academic, Christian ex–oil millionaire), were adamantly opposed to our participation. They ordered the professors to give double zeros to anyone missing mid–term exams that coincided with the timing of the planned march. We were also told that without parental permission, we would not be allowed to participate in the event, at the risk of expulsion.

In my case, Dad was way up in some remote place in northwest Canada speaking at churches and was difficult to locate and contact. Eventually, while I was in the office of the Dean of Student Affairs, my dad could finally be reached by telephone. The Dean gave him an overview of our plans, indicating the 'concerns' of the college administration, and also indicating that his permission would be required for me to participate. Dad asked to talk to me. I basically told him that the aims of the civil rights march in Selma, to me, were consistent with Christian principles, the social message of Jesus to oppose injustice, as well as with the aims of the ongoing civil rights campaigns led by the minister, Dr. Martin Luther King. I think my Dad's response caught the Dean by surprise. He forcefully indicated to her that he was very proud of the initiative that we were taking to participate in the Selma event, and that he gave me his unqualified support and backing. Our professors, in turn, indicated that they would refuse to give us zeros on our exams, and that make–up exams were okay. My sociology professor even asked me to write essays on my observations and experiences once we returned, in lieu of a test.

In the end, we drove day and night in two cars, arriving early in the day before the event. We stayed in the houses of relatives of my African American friend transfer student (a Moody Bible Institute graduate), listened to speeches and engaged in discussions with others. Local police drove around snapping pictures of the participants. The next day, after crossing the bridge in a long procession of marchers, we returned back over the bridge and headed north for the long drive to Greenville. Ironically, on observing the success of and national support for the march, the college administration quickly reversed course and staged a Thursday chapel focused on our participation in the march. The president indicated how proud the College was that Greenville students had gone to participate in the event.

Many years later when my son was in eighth grade at the mission-operated Mountain View International School in Salatiga, Central Java, Indonesia, his African American social studies teacher led a class session on the U.S. civil rights movement. As a part of the class session he showed a brief film on U.S. civil rights history that included scenes from the Selma, Alabama march. When his teacher talked about the importance of the Selma march, my son, David, surprised the classroom by stating that "My dad was there!" Thanks, Dad. Your legacy continues across generations.

Film Producer and His Photography Legacy

My dad had a special interest in and indulgence for photography, both black and white still photographs initially, supplemented later by color photography. He had good and multiple cameras, some of which he typically bought secondhand, and passed on to me at an early age. At his house there are albums full of his black and white photographs from the 1940s and later. He maintained this interest until late in his life, although he later moved on to simpler, more modern and even automatic cameras.

I carried on this tradition during three years of Ph.D. dissertation research, often sporting three SLR cameras for special agricultural and irrigation ceremonies, harvest festivals and multiple wedding events (black and white prints, color prints, color slides). Both of my children have carried on with this legacy and tradition with their own serious Nikon cameras.

Dad also owned movie as well as slide projectors that he used to show films, both while in the U.S. and later in India. During his period of advanced studies between 1948–1952, when we did not go to movies or have access to television, Dad would bring home and show black and white World War II documentary films that he borrowed from the University of Cincinnati and public libraries.

During his eight-year initial stay in India in the 1940s, including the war years, Dad also had a movie camera that he used to take moving pictures of multiple amazing events and places. Eventually he produced a two-hour movie which he took back to the U.S. and used for deputation purposes. In the movie Mom, my older sister Christine, and I saw coverage of the annual Magh Mela festival held in Allahabad. During the month-long Allahabad mela, and especially on peak days, millions of pilgrims came to the confluence of the Ganges and Jumna rivers (the Sangam) to wash away their sins, including throngs of thousands of sadhus marching naked. He had movies of some of his treks to remote Himalayan mountain pilgrimage locations and sacred bathing sites, and pictures of all kinds of pilgrims and local residents that he met along the way. He had pictures of hundreds of Shiite Muslim men marching in procession striking their backs with swords with blood flowing everywhere in remembrance of the killing of Ali. These represent only a few of the many events, themes and topics covered in his film. Unfortunately, when I asked Dad in his later years what had happened to the film, he had no memory of where it might be stored, so the film is lost forever.

Athletics and Sports

Dad did not have an active interest in sports and, apparently as a child, did not also actively participate in sports. I can contrast this to my own active participation in my school years and beyond in multiple sports, along with that of my children. I have always been an avid sports fan. By contrast, my mom used to play basketball in high school, and retained an interest in and used to watch the Indiana Pacers on TV. Despite this lack of interest, he would at times make attempts to come into the room while we were watching TV and sit down—staring intently at the TV screen and occasionally making odd comments—that I/we would get a kick out of. At Woodstock High School in India I was very active in sports, participating on the high school varsity teams in softball, soccer, volleyball and, in particular, track and field where I was a sprinter and long jumper. Dad never once had a chance to watch me play in any sports because some of these sports occurred during periods when Dad was not in the mountains but back down on the plains in Allahabad, or traveling.

That being said, during trips to Greenwood and Indianapolis, over multiple years, I used to always arrange with Dad to book sporting events in advance, and would take my kids and Dad to attend at least one Pacer game a year, an occasional ice hockey game, one Indianapolis Colts football game and, on one occasion, a Cincinnati Reds baseball game. In all of these occasions I would buy a ticket for Dad and he would always enjoy attending.

Dad did not know how to swim, and I often told him that in writing his autobiography, he should bring this fact up. I don't think this and other recommendations made much of an impression on him. I do recall, however, a four-to five-day hike that we once took while staying in the hill station of Landour, Mussoorie, in the Himalayan Mountains, to a government forest reserve in a valley 18 miles away. I also remember our making a small pool by moving boulders to dam up part of a stream, with Dad enthusiastically splashing around like a half-drowned puppy.

My final memory, in this regards, was when we were sailing on a Dutch freighter during early February 1953, just off the coast of Europe, in the midst of the worst storm in the North Atlantic during the last 60 years. During the storm, the dykes of Holland were flooded and over 2,000 people drowned in the Zuider Zee area of Zeeland. Dad was outside on the deck at night, fearlessly filming the storm and admiring God's power, with huge waves crashing over the bow of the ship, despite the fact that he could not swim. We were all relieved to see him come back inside.

Himalayan Mountain Trekker

The one exception to Dad's lack of interest in sporting events relates to his love of hiking in the Himalayan Mountains in India, particularly in his younger years. When I was in school 2,000 meters up in the Himalayan mountains, Dad and Mom would come up during the period of May-July (Mom would stay a month longer) and we would live in the mission cottage named Tipperary. Dad would often hike with our dog, Snooks, to engage in prayer and meditation, four to five miles out along the trail, and return by early evening.

One of the more interesting things that Dad did during the 1942-1944 period was to take two-to three-week pilgrimage treks to remote pilgrimage sites. In particular, he trekked to three of the four sacred sources of the Ganges. As I recall, the sacred river source pilgrimage sites that he visited were Jumnotri, Gangotri, and Kedarnath. In recent years he could not recall the specific details of his treks, nor which three of the four Ganga River sources that he hiked to other than Kedarnath, where there is a photographic record. He often trekked with a friend or two, meeting sadhus and pilgrims along the way. The black and white photos show him with a walking cane, khaki shorts and shirt, and a pith helmet. Some of the sites ended in abruptly rising steep snow slopes and ridges.

Widely Known as a Man of Prayer

I am very aware of the amount of attention and time Dad spent and invested in prayer. This is evidenced by the number of widely circulated books on prayer that he wrote during the active writing phase of his life, post OMS presidency. To many, my father was viewed as a spiritual prayer warrior.

In this context, I would like to cite a personal anecdote involving my mom and dad and the family of one of my closest friends, whom I have known over the last 40 years from Indonesia. My friend is Harbrindijit Singh Dillon (known as Lali among his close friends), an Indonesian of Sikh ancestry. When Lali and his family were at Cornell University in Ithaca, New York, and we were both writing up our doctoral dissertations, Lali was temporarily living in the house of a professor on sabbatical leave. At that time, Dad and Mom visited and had dinner at the house where Lali and his family were staying. Following our post-dinner conversations, as my parents, my wife Retno, and young daughter Santi, and I were preparing to leave, Dad put his arms around us and offered a short prayer of blessing for the two families. In the years that have followed, Lali has frequently repeated to me and others how much that moment meant, and how much he admired Dad. He would always ask me to convey his greetings to Dad. Lali would always say to my friends that you could look into Dad's warm eyes and observe his friendly, calm smile, and know that you were in the presence of a holy man and saint, a man of prayer, whose life's trajectory was to do good for others and leave the world a better place. Just before I left Indonesia, when I informed Lali of Dad's passing, three months short of 100 years old, Lali repeated and asked me to convey his appreciation and admiration of Dad and his life on his behalf.

Thanks and Appreciation: Free Methodist Church and OMS

I closed my tribute comments expressing my family's appreciation, and that also of my siblings, of the many kindnesses, love and care shown to Hilda and all of us by the OMS and Free Methodist church community in the arrangements made and the handling of the memorial service. I am so appreciative of the OMS and Free Methodist communities with whom my dad and mom were privileged to live their lives and share friendships over multiple decades. Dad, observing his memorial service from on high, clearly was overjoyed and delighted, a life well-lived.

John Wesley **Duewel**, oldest child
Semarang, Indonesia

Wesley and John Duewel

Family Tributes

Wesley, Hilda, John, Retno, Santi and Tim Gaul, and David Duewel

Four Generations of Duewels

Santi (Duewel) Gaul Tribute

What I will always appreciate about my grandpa...what he passed on to my father...and what was, in turn, instilled in me, is this: a love for learning and holding oneself to the highest academic standard, and a dedication to hard work for something you believe in. Years ago, when I sent my masters dissertation to my grandpa to read, he wrote me a letter, and told me that it was "*a real Duewel piece of work*" – for me, this was the highest compliment. My drive, my yearning to continue learning and improving, to work hard at the work that I love and for the people I love, and to help people – I know I can trace all these qualities back to my grandpa. I was my grandparents' only granddaughter, but I was never held to a different standard than the boys, only ever encouraged to be the best version of myself I could be. I only hope I can continue to pass on these qualities inherited from my grandpa, to my son.

Santi Duewel **Gaul**, granddaughter
Columbus, OH

David Duewel Tribute

Grandpa had such an adventurous, healthy, and full life. We should all hope we have the same.

David Duewel, grandson
London, United Kingdom

Family Tributes

Tribute to Dad

Dad was not as constant a presence in my life or, I think, the lives of John and Darlene as was our mother, Betty. She often had to shoulder a heavy load alone, while Dad's focus was his work and ministry, which are being abundantly acknowledged here today. Still, we always knew that Dad loved us deeply.

Dad was an only child, and I suspect often a lonely child. He never experienced the rough and tumble of siblings and maybe at times even friends, as his mother, my grandmother, was often ill. His parents held him to very high, perhaps impossibly high, standards. He surely found those standards onerous at times. All his life, I think, he held very high standards for himself and those he held dear. He had a burden to share his Christian witness with the world, as everyone here knows. Later in life it often seemed to me that Dad had time for little else. I wanted to tell him that God didn't expect him to save the world all by himself!

As a young boy Dad had a beloved canine companion named Teddy. I asked Dad to tell me what he had dreamed about once. He reported that he had dreamed about Teddy. Later in India we all grew to love Snooks. And I know Dad had a dog between Teddy and Snooks, name forgotten, who was jealous of Mom. It makes me happy to think that Teddy, Snooks, and company gave Dad unconditional acceptance and love, with no standards attached.

Dad had a very kind heart, as did my mother. I remember no harsh words or harsh discipline during my childhood, although of course we children knew when we had disappointed our parents. I remember happy family times with Dad when we were young, from pillow fights to family games and outings to rides on the back of Dad's motorcycle to the shopping area in Allahabad, India, where we lived. Our family's favorite store there was the bookstore, where we each got to buy a book. Dad always encouraged reading and learning. When John and I became old enough to decide we knew way more than he did, Dad kept encouraging us.

My dear friend Sue Oiler Dowse, formerly of the OMS, called last week to tell me how much she admired Dad. She said he was always "approachable, kind, and human." She recalled a time at OMS when he got down on his hands and knees to push a toy car along with his nose. It was a contest having something to do with Indy 500, I guess. Thanks for your words, Sue. How nice to hear that Dad could still let his inner child out to play.

Thanks also to so many of you present who have said kind things to me, John, and Darlene about Dad and have helped plan this service, provide meals, and contributed in other ways toward celebrating Dad's life.

Recently Dad's life became very circumscribed by frailty and illness, demanding constant care, mostly from Hilda. We children cannot thank you enough, Hilda. Despite his infirmities, you have kept our dear father well cared for and happy. God bless you!

In recent days when I called, Dad could hear little of what I said on the phone as he became very hard of hearing. But he always sounded cheerful and appreciative. Recently he started to call me sweetheart. How that endearment has touched my heart.

Last week Ed and I attended our usual monthly poetry gathering in our small town in West Virginia. I usually read three poems from the Writer's Almanac, which I receive online daily. At this gathering, on the day after

Dad died, I read two poems from the almanac and then one of Dad's. I'll close by reading the last verse of that poem, The Hand That Holds You.

The hand enfolding space and time
In love so full and free.
The hand of love that blesses all
To all eternity,
The Father's gentle, loving hand—
So faithful, constant, true—
God's own right hand of perfect love—
That hand is holding you!

Ruth **Christine** Duewel **Zahniser**, middle child
Shepherdstown, WV

Justin Zahniser Tribute

Everyone is quite familiar with Grandpa Wesley's incredible life of service. However, not everyone outside of his family has experienced his rarely employed, but delightfully mischievous grin. His soul was bigger than a body could contain, which may be why he shared it so readily with the world.

Justin Zahniser, grandson
Silver Spring, MD

Family Tributes

Eric Zahniser Tribute

Grandpa Wesley was always present in the moment. I felt his presence when I was with him in a very positive way. When he shook my hand and we looked at each other in the eyes, I could sense his inner strength and the fortitude of his soul in a very real way.

He was passionate about his vocation and his calling, and I think that contributed to his vitality and his long life.

I had reflected on that twice in the past year or two, due to other people of whom I had encountered or been aware. Don Lorenzo Servitje, who founded the company, Grupo Bimbo, for whom I work, is 97 years old and still involved with the business. Until this year, he came to the office most days. People always say that when he speaks to you, you feel he is fully focused on you 100% present.

I always have thought Grandpa Wesley was the exact same way. I remember he was talking to a stranger at the airport in Florida when we had flown down there about twelve years ago for a family event. He was totally in the moment and so clearly listening and talking to this man and not thinking of anything else.

Another parallel that made me reflect on this was when I was reading an interview with a Jewish musician named Matisyahu, and he was describing a Rabbi at a synagogue he attended in Brooklyn. He was talking about how intense this man was about praying and attending even though he was barely physically able to make it to the synagogue. He said you could tell he was a "real deal holy" man. And I thought, yes that sounds like Grandpa Wesley.

Grandpa was a real deal holy man. He was strong. He was intense. I could tell every time I spoke with him or was with him in person that he cared so deeply about me and about life in general. I could tell that he really felt life in his heart.

I will cherish his memory, and I'm proud of him. Grandpa was loved and admired by so many people. I will always remember his strength, warmth, and clarity of purpose.

Eric and Katie **Zahniser**, grandson
Philadelphia, PA

Family Tributes

My Dad

I want to begin by thanking Hilda for the wonderful care she gave my dad in the last seven years of his life. As friends, co-workers and acquaintances have expressed their sympathy to me, I have told them that he had the best care possible. The most expensive and well-staffed facility wouldn't have given him the quality of life that he had at home with Hilda. Thank you, Hilda, for faithfully serving and ministering to Dad. Because of you, he was able to spend his later years in the comfort of his own home with home-cooked meals and loving care giving. I also want to express my appreciation to the OMS staff, dear friends of my parents at the West Morris Street Free Methodist Church, and others who may have contributed to this celebration of my dad's life. I also want to thank everyone who has taken the time and effort to come be with us here today.

We have heard several tributes to my dad with regards to his ministry, so I thought I would share some interesting facts about my dad apart from his work. As I was growing up, one of his favorite treats was malted milk balls. He would often keep a stash of them in one of the side drawers in his desk. Fortunately, I wasn't tempted to sneak any, because I didn't really like them. He also enjoyed Hostess Ding Dongs, and the turnover-shaped Hostess Cherry Pies. Of course, homemade cherry pie was his favorite. Full stomachs led to naps. After weekday lunches, Dad had the uncanny ability to fall asleep immediately and wake up refreshed 15 or 20 minutes later. Not only were Dad's naps quick, they could be loud. We children would wait as his snoring would steadily increase in volume. Then, he would reach the climax, following which he would suddenly awake with a start and a sheepish smile.

Family Tributes

Dad appreciated nature and history. On cross-country jaunts to OMS conferences and vacations, we would stop and hike in national parks, visit national monuments, and sightsee other points of interest. If we happened to be going in the vicinity of one of our OMS supporters, we knew that meant a stop at a phone booth at a gas station or other location. Mom and I would sit in the car, while Dad made the calls and expressed his appreciation for the supporter's prayer and financial support. It got warm sitting in a non-air-conditioned car in the summer time, so I'm sure there were times when I prayed that some of those dear people would not be home.

Dad had a sense of humor. As a pre-teen, I remember my dad mouthing the words to a record on which the 1947 song "I'm My Own Grandpa" was sung. Dad performed it at some OMS staff event here at Headquarters. The song was written by Dwight Latham and Moe Jaffe and sung by Lonzo and Oscar. It was about a man who, through an unlikely (but legal) combination of marriages, becomes stepfather to his own stepmother—that is, tacitly dropping the "step" modifiers, he becomes his own grandfather. Dad dressed up and put some humorous actions to the words as he mouthed them to the recording. The song had various stanzas but always returned to the refrain "I'm my own Grandpa." As a kid, I thought it very funny to see this side of my dad doing something silly and humorous. On one of Dad's trips to New Zealand, he was participating in a fellowship meal at a church. As in Britain, certain words in New Zealand have different meanings than they do in the U.S. In New Zealand "nursing a baby" can mean taking care of it. As Dad was sitting and visiting at the fellowship meal, a woman came up to him and asked him if he would "nurse" the baby. I'm sure Dad had a twinkle in his eye when his response to her was "*With God all things are possible*." He always enjoyed telling this story to people. When taking family pictures, instead of saying the typical 1, 2, 3, he opted to say –

elephants, giraffes, monkeys. We all knew MONKEYS meant smile. Dad liked coming up with his own pronunciation of certain words. Instead of saying "syllable," he liked to pronounce it syl-LA-ble. He also would get a mischievous smile when he would inform us how the word Duewel was pronounced in German – DE-vil.

In past days when Dad frequently traveled out of the U.S., we could count on a Christmas gift from a country where he had been. One of his yearly Christmas traditions was to shop the blue light special at K-Mart. The blue light special was a small window of time, between 10 p.m. and midnight on Christmas Eve. Dad liked bargains, and felt especially successful when he found a really cheap deal. Following his midnight jaunt, he would stay up late wrapping and labeling presents. One Christmas tradition Dad faithfully performed every year was the reading of the Christmas story. Then, he would don a different hat, literally, a red Santa hat, read the gift labels with great fanfare and pass out the presents.

One of Dad's legacies to his family was his evening prayers. He and Hilda would spend part of the evening praying for family members, friends, and other needs that they knew about. One evening when I was staying the night with Dad and Hilda, I sat in on the family prayers. As Dad's memory faded a bit, he would repeat himself during the prayer time. That night I felt well-covered because Dad prayed for our family a total of four times – each time petitioning with great fervency. I smiled to myself, but felt sure the fourfold repetition didn't matter to God. Thank you, Dad! I know God has used those prayers to bless each of us in various ways.

We will miss Dad, but I'm sure that he would assure us how wonderful it is to be free of the physical encumbrances that were weighing him down and which made life on earth such an effort in his last days. Well done, Dad, we love you.

Esther **Darlene** Duewel **Rueger**, youngest child
Lawrenceburg, IN

Jonathan Rueger Tribute

I will always remember Grandpa for his unwavering dedication to his work and his deeply felt compassion for the people he was called to serve. It was great to spend holidays with him. He was generous to provide financial assistance through college and his prayer support for me. But the character traits I will recall most fondly were the humor and grace with which he responded to Christmas pranks.

Jonathan Rueger, grandson
Hollywood, CA

Jason Rueger Tribute

It was always enjoyable to have a chance to talk and carry on a conversation with him. What I will always remember most fondly about Grandpa was his smile and his funny sense of humor. I often asked, "*Grandpa, how did you sleep*?" whenever he would come over to visit. His response was always the same, "*I didn't stay awake to find out*," said with a twinkle in his eye and a smile on his face. In addition to his sense of humor, Grandpa was also deeply dedicated and passionate about his work and calling, something that will always challenge me as I navigate the waters of career and calling in my own life. He was such a Godly example to me while I growing up. The Christmas tradition of reading the story of the birth of Jesus is something I intend to carry on in my household when the time comes. I hope that I can say I was as good a Grandpa to my grandchildren as you were to me. Grandpa, I am glad you are now in the presence of your loving Savior, fully at peace and rest.

Jason Rueger, grandson
Lawrenceburg, IN

A Life Well Lived – My Cousin

Last week I attended the memorial service of my cousin, Wesley Duewel, who passed away at the age of 99. When he was five playing in his sandbox, he heard God call him to be a missionary in India. He was faithful to that call and for the past 75 years, he gave his life to the cause of Christ and world missions.

Although he is well known because of the 2.5 million of his 10 books that are now in 58 languages, those who met him recognized that he lived by the words he used to sign his letters: "*All for Jesus*."

Rev. Mark Wilson writing about the passing of Wesley Duewel, told that seven years ago his congregation was transformed as they went through Dr. Duewel's book *Ablaze for God.* They invited him, then age 92, to Hayward, Wisconsin so he could share his heart and pray with them. To their delight, he accepted the invitation. Rev. Wilson wrote:

"Obtaining special permission, I eagerly awaited Dr. Duewel's arrival at Gate A-19 of Minneapolis International Airport. His plane landed, and a long line of passengers debarked – but no Wesley Duewel.

"The last stragglers came out of the tunnel, but there was still no sign of my special guest. I checked with the agent who radioed back into the plane, and grunted, 'He's coming. He's coming.'

"Finally, three flight attendants emerged from the jet bridge, and they were all wiping away tears. One approached me, 'Are you the one waiting for that precious little old man back there?' she blubbered. 'He was just praying for us! It was so beautiful! I have never felt such love in all my life!'

"I marveled. This holy man was so filled with God's presence and anointing that it automatically overflowed to everybody he met along the way."

"Blessed are the dead who die in the Lord ... "they will rest from their labor, for their deeds will follow them!" (Revelation 14:13)

Aletha Hinthorn, cousin and author
Come to the Fire, Leawood, KS

My Savior First of All (verses 1, 2, 3, 4)

When my life-work is ended, and I cross the swelling tide,
When the bright and glorious morning I shall see;
I shall know my Redeemer when I reach the other side,
And His smile will be the first to welcome me.

Refrain:
I shall know Him, I shall know Him,
And redeemed by His side I shall stand,
I shall know Him, I shall know Him
By the print of the nails in His hand.

Oh, the soul-thrilling rapture when I view His blessed face,
And the luster of His kindly beaming eye;
How my full heart will praise Him for the mercy, love, and grace,
That prepare for me a mansion in the sky.

Oh, the dear ones in glory, how they beckon me to come,
And our parting at the river I recall;
To the sweet vales of Eden they will sing my welcome home;
But I long to meet my Savior first of all.

Thro' the gates to the city in a robe of spotless white,
He will lead me where no tears will ever fall;
In the glad song of ages I shall mingle with delight;
But I long to meet my Savior first of all.

Fanny J. Crosby, 1820–1915

Evangelical Church of India Tributes

Introduction to OMS India[1]

India, not the Orient, was the first missions' focus of Charles E. Cowman, cofounder of The Oriental Missionary Society. Cowman began to think God was calling him to India. And very likely he would have gone had wife Lettie's health been sufficiently robust to tolerate India's demanding environment. Though God sent the Cowmans to the Orient, they did not forget India, but prayed fervently that her millions would one day come to know Jesus as Savior and Lord.

In July 1939, fifteen years after Cowman's death in 1924, no doubt divinely orchestrated partly in answer to Wesley's prayer, the OMS board voted to enter India. The first team of seven, including Wesley and Betty Duewel, landed in Bombay, in February 1941, followed a few weeks later by Eugene and Esther Erny, who were reassigned from China, to give experienced leadership to the new field.

The initial ministry outreach was launched in the 1940's and the subsequent ministries, including the development and expansion of the Evangelical Church of India (ECI), which God raised up through the joint efforts of OMS personnel and Indian nationals who, for the most part, were graduates of the OMS-established Bible seminaries. It was at Allahabad, one of the first major Bible seminaries, which Dr. Duewel contributed significantly in establishing and leading.

Nevertheless, the first 10 years of OMS' involvement in India was very difficult and there was very little sense of fruitfulness or reward. The growth and development of the ECI was slow, starting with one church

---

[1] Extracted from the unpublished article on **OMS India History** written by Rev. Rudy Rabe in 2000.

every year for the first 25 years, then increasing to one church every month over the next 25 years, then one church every week over the next ten years, then three churches every week over the next ten years. Today the ECI consists of over 16,896 churches, a membership of over 750,000 and growing at the rate of approximately 4 ½ churches weekly. The ECI's own mission effort, the Indian Missionary Movement (IMM), supports over 800 indigenous workers serving among the unreached tribal groups. The ECI Centennial goal is to establish 100,000 churches with ten million members. What's made the difference? We trace it to the breakthrough prayer effort led by Dr. Duewel, along with the deeply embedded prayer habit sown deep within the spiritual DNA of ECI that characterized those foundational years and continues to manifest itself in ECI throughout India. The following tributes from ECI leaders hint at just how much influence Dr. Duewel continues to wield in the corporate history of ECI.

Dr. Duewel flanked by Bishops Ezra Sargunam and Sundar Singh

Evangelical Church of India Tributes

Evangelical Church of India (ECI)

We are saddened to hear about the passing of the missionary veteran and man of prayer Dr. Wesley Duewel. The Evangelical Church of India owes a great deal of debt to Dr. Duewel for his 25 years of service during the early days of his ministry. His love for India and the Indian people will always be remembered. Pastors and believers of ECI express their deep condolences at this time of bereavement and grief to the family members.

I was amazed when I spoke with OMS Leaders, especially Dr. Duewel on Skype, some months back. His memory was so vivid. He spoke very clearly, thanking God that the missionaries had deferred the decision to send me back home when I came to join the Madras Bible Seminary at the age of 16, as I was too young to attend the seminary.

With prayers,
Dr. M. **Ezra Sargunam**, Father-Bishop
Dr. D. **Sundar Singh**, Bishop-President
Rev. S. Duraiswamy, International Partnership Liaison
Evangelical Church of India, Chennai, Tamil Nadu, India

Allahabad Bible Seminary (ABS)

It was with sadness that I announced, Dr. Wesley Duewel, one of the early Principals of Allahabad Bible Seminary and the author of *Touch the World through Prayer* and numerous other books, entered into his eternal rest on the night of March 5, 2016. Dr. Wesley Duewel was a man of many peers, but few equals. Dr. Duewel was the President Emeritus of One Mission Society, formerly OMS International, the founding mission of Allahabad Bible Seminary. We appreciate your prayers for members of the bereaved family.

On the evening of March 8, 2016, we had a Memorial Thanksgiving service as we gave thanks to God for the life of His dear saint Rev. Dr. Wesley Duewel. The entire ABS community, the faculty, staff and students gathered in the ABS chapel. Dr. Ashish Chrispal shared a meaningful devotion. Rev. J. Sundara Raj and I shared about the life of Dr. Duewel and his commitment to the Lord, to the Church and missions. We at ABS value and treasure the great heritage left behind by the founding fathers of Allahabad Bible Seminary and very especially the life of Dr. Duewel. I had the privilege to be one of his interpreters at the prayer conference conducted at Allahabad in November 1991. We send our condolences to the bereaved family.

Rev. **Sethna Pervez,** Professor
Allahabad Bible Seminary, Allahabad, Uttar Pradesh, India

Evangelical Church of India Tributes

Evangelical Theological Academy (ETA)

It is a privilege to be associated with men of great faith of OMS. I have been much encouraged by Dr. Wesley Duewel. However, I am sad to learn of Dr. Duewel's passing into glory. Some years ago I had the privilege of praying with him. He prayed for my lower limbs to be strengthened, as I had developed severe numbness. Hallelujah, I was immediately healed of my illness! His prayer for me was so effective that I survived all these years. He earnestly prayed for me and for others. While teaching ECI pastors, I gave away some of his books, such as *Mighty Prevailing Prayer*, to many so that they are blessed today. He, although absent from the body, yet speaks to all of us. He, along with a host of other OMS missionaries, are heroes of faith, they attempted great things for God. He has left a great legacy for the Indian pastors, particularly ECI pastors to practice his theology of prayer. He has told us that we can, *Touch the World through Prayer*. Also, we can overcome and be conquerors as Christ the victor has conquered. Still I have to learn much from this great man of faith.

Best wishes and prayers,
Rev. Dr. **Samuel Jayakumar**, Ph.D., Director
Evangelical Theological Academy, Chennai, Tamil Nadu, India

Karnataka Bible Seminary (KBS)

Thank you for giving this information. His heart for India will never be forgotten in our lifetime. We pray for the family left behind.

Rev. **John Harris,** Principal
Karnataka Bible Seminary, Karnataka, India

Evangelical Church of India Tributes

Kolkata Diocese and Calcutta Bible Seminary (CBS)

We of the ECI Kolkata Diocese and CBS deeply convey our condolence to the bereaved family and OMS. We are thankful to Dr. Wesley Duewel for all that he has done for OMS in India and the planting of ECI churches in India. I had the privilege to listen to his pious and powerful messages few times in India. We will miss him. We do pray for you the entire family.

With prayer and love,
Rev. **Isaac Mangalraj**, Associate Bishop–Administrator
ECI Kolkata Diocese–ECI CBS, Kolkata, West Bengal, India

Madras Theological Seminary and College (MTCS)

Kindly pass on the condolence message of MTSC family to the bereaved family of Dr. Wesley Duewel. We fondly remember his time at MTSC to teach to the students and also to conduct training sessions for the pastors. He was a man of prayer who had a great burden for India. On March 8, we observed a special time of prayer for Dr. Duewel's family, and also thanked God for his contribution to God's ministries at large. We hope his son received his exit permit from Indonesia and reached U.S. in time to attend the funeral service. Thank you for informing us about the live streaming of Dr. Wesley Duewel's funeral service tonight. We will try to watch the same. Dr. Duewel's family and the entire OMS staff are in our prayers. Heb. 11:4 "*He* (Dr. Wesley Duewel) *being dead still speaks*."

With prayers,
Rev. Dr. J. A. **David Onesimu,** Principal
Madras Theological Seminary and College, Chennai, Tamil Nadu, India

Allahabad Bible Seminary

Madras Theological Seminary and College

Calcutta Bible Seminary

'Tis Jesus! Heaven Has Begun!

Oh, what a thrilling glory sight!
Heav'n's massive gate is gleaming white;
On either side the angels stand
To welcome to the glory land,
Each face aglow with holy love—
The welcome band to heav'n above.

The herald angels' trumpet blare
Announces through heav'n's jasper air
That Wesley enters through the gate.
They summon loved ones who await.
Along the street of crystal gold
What scenes of glory now unfold!

Beside the spacious avenue
Sights never glimpsed by mortal view—
Celestial parks on either side
With walks and fountains, gardens wide
Abloom with iridescent flow'rs
And trees of life in leafy bow'rs.

Then rad'ant saints from either side
Come smiling with arms open wide.
They greet but quickly fall in line
To 'scort to scenes e'en more divine.
New vistas on each side amaze;
The entire city gleams ablaze!

The escort angels gladly lead
The happy throng with quickened speed.
Their trumpet melodies resound;
Expectancy and joys abound.
On down the heav'nly street they press
With e'er increasing eagerness.

At last they reach the central square
Where wait new joys beyond compare.
Before them, Lo! The throne at last!
Circled by angel throng so vast!
Thinks Wesley, Oh! How can it be
That I my Lord at last shall see!

Lo! On the throne a form divine
From which all glory seems to shine!
Yes, look! Behold the human face
Adorned with glory, love, and grace!
'Tis Jesus! Still the Son of Man!
'Tis Jesus! Oh, what God has planned!

'Tis Jesus! Rising from the throne!
For Wesley now sees Him alone!
Forgotten—all who round him stand;
Forgotten—rad'ant angel band!
His eyes see only Jesus' face!
Christ's holy features he can trace!

He gazes, lost in ecstacy.
How can such blessing be for me!
Then Jesus reaches out His hand

And gives him strength so he can stand.
He calls him! Yes, it is his name!
How can he ever be the same?

'Tis Jesus! Face to face with Him!
Now all earth's trials pale and dim!
'Tis Jesus! He's by Jesus' side!
'Tis Jesus! His arms open wide!
'Tis Jesus! Hear him say, "Well done!"
'Tis Jesus! Heaven has begun!

Wesley L. Duewel, February 11, 1987
Written for the funeral of Dr. Eugene A. Erny
Slightly adapted by Jason Campbell for this occasion

Nusantara Evangelical Church, Leadership 2015

Nusantara Evangelical Church Tributes

Introduction to OMS South Pacific Ministry[1]

The launching of OMS ministry in the South Pacific and the establishment of both the Nusantara Bible Seminary (NBS) and the Nusantara Evangelical Christian Church (NEC), and today's second branch seminary, the Nusantara Theological College (NTC), was the outgrowth of Dr. Wesley Duewel actions, who as OMS President at the time, was involved in the initial survey trip in 1967. Over the next seven years, under his leadership and influenced by his spiritual guidance, key mission leaders cast the vision, launched the outreach, nurtured the earliest national church leaders, formed the initial constitution and by-laws, and established the ecclesiastical foundation upon which NEC was established.

In contrast with the OMS ministry in India, the NEC grew quite rapidly at the outset. In 1974 the first year five congregations were established and formed the basis upon which NEC was officially registered and recognized by the Republic of Indonesia. In March of the second year, the first NEC general conference was conducted to formally launch the denomination, elect the first Indonesian chairman, and formulate the first NEC-OMS joint-working agreement. In 1976 OMS leaders in conjunction with NEC leaders set the first ten-year goals of starting 200 new congregations with 15,000 total members. Those were ambitious plans considering they were formed and implemented in the heart of the largest, most populace Islamic nation in the world.

Today, the NEC consists of 120 congregations spread across the archipelago located in every province, continuing to be as active in

---

[1] Extracted and synthesized from the **OMS Indonesia History** written by David Dick in 2000.

propagating the Gospel as federal laws and local restrictions permit. NEC leadership continue to express their sense of indebtedness to Dr. Wesley Duewel for the vision and energy he devoted to helping launch the ministry in their *'land–sea'* homeland.

Nusantara Bible Seminary, Malang, East Java

Nusantara Evangelical Church Tributes

PINTA Foundation

On behalf of the entire management and staff of the ***Foundation for Propagation of the Good News throughout the Archipelago*** (PINTA), we express our sincerest condolences at the home going of Rev. Dr. Wesley Duewel into our Heavenly Father's presence. We believe that Dr. Duewel has already received the most beautiful part of the Father's promise in that He would provide a glorious place at our Heavenly Father's side.

We pray that our steadfast loving Father will continue to pour forth His peace and comfort upon the entire extended family left behind, and that you will continue to emulate, or exemplify, your loved one's life and service throughout the remainder of your lives.

Rev. **Firman** Hartadi, S.Th., MA., Chairman
PINTA Foundation, Malang, Indonesia

Nusantara Evangelical Church

On behalf of the greater ***Nusantara Evangelical Church Synod*** family, we lift up praise and thanksgiving to the Lord Jesus expressly because of the love of the Lord Jesus Christ, Dr. Wesley Duewel was called to our Father in Heaven. We also give thanks because Dr. Duewel has been an extraordinary instrument used by God to grow and bless the people of many nations, especially Indonesia. We pray for the family that God may bless you with the power and strength of the Lord.

Amen
Rev. **Agus** Santoso, M.Th., Chairman
Nusantara Evangelical Church Synod, Malang, Indonesia

Nusantara Evangelical Church Tributes

Nusantara Bible Seminary

Precious in the sight of the Lord is the death of His saints (Psalm 116:15).

Dear Mrs. Duewel and family,

On behalf of the whole family of the Nusantara Bible Seminary in Malang, Indonesia: I would like to express our deep sympathy and condolences to the family of Dr. Wesley Duewel. May God, our Father, bestow you with strength and comfort during this difficult time.

With deep regards,
Rev. **Francis** Nawa Hoke, M.Div., M.Th., President
Nusantara Bible Seminary, Malang, Indonesia

Nusantara Theological College of Salatiga

The staff, employees, and the family-at-large of the ***Nusantara Theological College*** of Salatiga would like to express our condolences on this occasion of the home calling of Rev. Dr. Wesley Duewel returning to the bosom of our Heavenly Father. Our prayers for you are that the Lord will give strength to the bereaved family and continuous joy in hope. May the Lord bless you.

With greetings and prayers,
Rev. **Puji** Swismanto, M.Th., Chairman
Nusantara Theological College, Salatiga, Indonesia

OMS South Pacific

Greetings in the love of Christ. Personally, I wish to convey my own sense of your deep loss at the home going of Rev. Dr. Wesley Duewel at the age of 99 into the loving embrace of our Heavenly Father. My prayers for you are that God may give strength and comfort to all the family, especially Mrs. Darlene Rueger and her children.

By means of this email, I also send condolences on behalf of the ***Foundation for the Propagation of the Good News throughout the Archipelago*** (PINTA), ***Nusantara Bible Seminary*** of Malang, ***Nusantara Theological College*** of Salatiga, and the entire ***Nusantara Evangelical Church of Indonesia*** as OMS partner institutions in Indonesia.

May God bless and comfort you,
Mrs. **Ika** Sutestri, Executive Secretary
OMS South Pacific, Malang, Indonesia

Nusantara Theological College, Salatiga, Central Java

How Blessed!

How blessed are the dead
Who served God mid earth's strife!
Now only glory lies ahead
And everlasting life.

How blessed there to stay
On heaven's glory shore,
To live in never-ending day
Where night and sin are o'er!

How blessed there to live
Where God's plans are fulfilled,
Where each can perfect service give
And do all God has willed!

How blessed to behold
The Savior's love-crowned face,
While God's eternal days unfold
More love and joy and grace!

How blessed, but not dead—
All live on heaven's shore—
Eternal blessing lies ahead
And life forevermore!

Wesley L. Duewel, November 25, 1967
Greenwood, IN

Introduction to OMS

One Mission Society, Inc. (known as The Oriental Missionary Society until February 1973) was founded as a faith mission in February 1901 by the late Rev. and Mrs. Charles E. Cowman, under a clear call from God and by the definite guidance of the Holy Spirit.

Written on the flyleaf of Charles Cowman's Bible in February 23, 1901 during his first journey to Japan, the OMS Founder penned the following words:

> *"The world is waiting yet to see what God can do through a consecrated soul. Not the world alone, but God Himself is waiting for one who would be more devoted to Him than any who have ever lived; who will be willing to be nothing that Christ may be all; who will grasp God's own purposes and taking His faith, His humility, His love will without hindering, continue to let God do exploits. There is no limit to what God can do with a man providing he does not touch the glory."*

OMS today stands on the shoulders of these founders and their successors, ten presidents in all over the last 115 years, who exemplified this kind of total surrender and entire sanctification. Starting with 1) Charles Cowman, followed by cofounder 2) Ernest A. Kilbourne, and then succeeded by former First Lady 3) Lettie Cowman, the first and only female president to date, and then 4) Eugene Erny, and his colleague and coworker 5) Wesley Duewel, who in turn was followed by 6) Everette Hunt, and 7) Edward Erny, and then 8) J.B. Crouse, Jr., 9) David Long, and today's tenth president 10) Robert Fetherlin.

OMS Tributes

Returning to the U.S. in 1964, Dr. Duewel had no intention of serving the Lord anywhere else but India. When the Board of OMS, then composed strictly of missionary peers, asked him to remain in the U.S. and serve as president at the international headquarters then located in Los Angeles, he accepted, *"with eyes wet with tears, ... since they were over me in the Lord."* He served as Second Vice President under his good friend Dr. Eugene Erny from 1965-1969, and was elected to succeed Dr. Erny and served as President from 1969-1982. During his tenure as president, the mission was greatly blessed and its outreach footprint expanded from 10 nations to 14 nations, including France, Indonesia, Philippines, and Spain. It's not uncommon for those members of the society who possess the collective memory of the Duewel presidency to think of that period as the 'Golden Era' of OMS contemporary history. In the following tributes, one can begin to understand what a significant and lasting impact Dr. Duewel had throughout his extended life and how much OMS has benefited from his long tenure with the organization for which he prayed for the better part of his 99 years.

In Tribute to Dr. Wesley Luelf Duewel

June 3, 1916 – March 5, 2016

Wesley Luelf Duewel was born in St. Charles, Missouri (a suburb of St. Louis), on Saturday, June 3, 1916, to God-honoring parents. His father was an evangelical pastor, Bible college president, and radio preacher. His mother was a godly woman with a deep and meaningful prayer life.

Wesley made his first profession of faith as a three-year-old, and soon thereafter was called by God, in the midst of his sandbox, to serve as a missionary to India. Throughout his life, he made many more life-changing decisions based on his increasing spiritual maturity that became evident in his heart, through his youth experiences; young adult education; professional preparation, up to and including, his election as the fifth president of OMS; and into his writing ministry following his presidency.

Wesley relied primarily on prayer and a sanctified sense of God's guidance as he met and married his first wife, Betty Raisch, in 1939. He discovered she had claimed the same life verse that he had: "*Enlarge the place of your tent; stretch your tent curtains wide, do not hold back; lengthen your cords, strengthen your stakes. For you will spread out to the right and to the left*" (Isaiah 54:2-3a). This promise served as a predictor of his eventual worldwide ministry.

During his time at God's Bible School, Wesley prayed earnestly for "an effectual door" to open for him to serve in India. By 1940, Wesley and Betty Duewel were among the first group of seven OMS missionaries who sailed for India.

OMS Tributes

Wesley and Betty underscored their work with prayer, and within two years, he helped found the Allahabad Bible Seminary. It was into this prayer-filled home that their son, John Wesley, was born in 1944. A daughter, Christine, joined the family two years later, and Darlene was included 10 years following.

As Wesley taught for 22 years at the seminary and served as its principal for 15, he and Betty carried a special burden for a praying, Spirit-filled church in India. After a quarter of a century, there was one church for every year they labored in love, with about 60 members each, and three small Bible schools in three states of India.

Returning for an OMS Board meeting in 1964, somewhere over the Pacific between Honolulu and Los Angeles, Wesley prayed again: *"Oh Lord, give us 1,000 people who will commit themselves to pray for 15 minutes a day for at least one year, specifically praying for our OMS India work."* God honored that prayer with 1,500 people from 32 nations who prayed over the next 12 months. It was a spiritual jump-start that broke through strongholds and opened the way for the Gospel to advance like never before.

The growth and development of the Evangelical Church of India (ECI) was slow, starting with one church every year for the first 25 years, then increasing to one church every month over the next 25 years, then one church every week over the next 10 years, then three churches every week over the next 10 years. Today, the ECI consists of more than 5,276 churches and 11,620 house churches, with a membership of more than 750,000 and growing at the rate of approximately 4½ churches weekly. There are also 13 Bible schools and seminaries. The deeply embedded prayer habit sown by Wesley and Betty during ECIs foundational years made the difference.

Dr. Duewel concluded his 13-year organizational leadership tenure in 1982 with a mission-wide emphasis called *"Decade of Harvest."* The next 10 years was one of the most fruitful eras of productivity One Mission Society had ever experienced. Following his presidency, Wesley was led to expand his writing ministry. His first major book, *Touch the World through Prayer,* has become a modern-day classic; circulation has reached nearly one million, and Dr. Duewel's nine subsequent publications have exceeded 2.5 million in circulation printed in 58 languages worldwide.

After Betty passed away in 2008, Wesley married his long-time secretary, Hilda Mae Johnecheck, who faithfully worked at his side in the Duewel Literature Trust, a not-for-profit, self-funded ministry.

"You can stand beside the great evangelists of our day; accompany any missionary to the remote reaches of the earth; contribute to the ministry of any pastor or evangelist in the world; or mediate the healing of Jesus Christ to the sick, ill, or faint of heart anywhere on the globe. Prayer is not the only thing you must do. It is the greatest thing you can do." Indeed, God enlarged and stretched, lengthened, and strengthened Wesley's ministry beyond anything that he, his parents, his wives, or his colleagues could ever have imagined. He was a man of many peers, but few equals.

Now to him who is able to do immeasurably more than all we ask or imagine, according to his power that is at work within us, to him be glory in the church and in Christ Jesus throughout all generations, for ever and ever! Amen (Ephesians 3:20–21).

OMS Tributes

Hilda, John, Christine, Darlene, as well as your children and grandchildren, be assured of our love and prayers for you during these days. The entire worldwide OMS family expresses our profound appreciation for Wesley's tireless service for God and his kingdom. We pray that the Holy Spirit's presence and comfort will uplift and strengthen you during these days of mourning your great loss. We know, however, that you do not grieve as those who have no hope. We rejoice with you, imagining how wonderful to Wesley's ears were the words spoken to him by Jesus, "*Well done, my good and faithful servant*." We rejoice with you in knowing that someday we will not only join Wesley in worshiping around the throne, but thousands and thousands of those whom he touched, through prayer, around the world.

For Esther and me personally, we had read some of Dr. Duewel's writings and heard about him. But it wasn't until we came to OMS in 2014 that we met him. We knew right away that we were in the presence of a great man of God, a spiritual giant! What a joy and honor it has been to pray and interact with him, to be inspired and challenged by him, and to see him finish well. The life he lived, and the way in which he lived it, will continue to be a poignant spiritual challenge to us and many others. We are so grateful for the life and ministry of Dr. Wesley Duewel.

We rejoice with you as his family and express deep gratitude to our Lord for a life extremely well lived for God's honor and glory,

Robert L. **Fetherlin**, President
One Mission Society, Greenwood, IN

OMS Tributes

OMS Board Resolution

RESOLVED, that the Board of Trustees of One Mission Society hereby records its deep appreciation for Dr. Wesley Duewel's dedicated service to God through the channels of One Mission Society; and

RESOLVED FURTHER, that the Board of Trustees extends sincere condolences to Hilda, John, Christine, Darlene and other family members who will greatly miss the presence of Dr. Wesley Duewel.

Robert L. **Fetherlin**, President
One Mission Society, Greenwood, IN

OMS Australia

We were saddened in spirit to hear of Wesley's home call. As we stand with you and pray that Jesus will be your comfort, strength and peace. Be assured that we will continue to support you before the throne of God's grace. Love from your brothers and sisters in Christ at OMS Australia.

Bernard Blumel, Chairman of the Board
OMS Australia

OMS Tributes

OMS East Asia

HIS GOOD AND FAITHFUL SERVANT: Lamenting the news that OMS icon Wesley Duewel was just promoted to glory...the very day I boarded the plane for China. Loved his wisdom, counsel, wit and friendship. What an incredible warrior . . . a Patton in spiritual warfare, an indefatigable scholar, a standard-bearer for sanctification, an insatiable encourager, and a missions genius who spent more time on his knees than most people spend eating . . . Impossible to fill his shoes....but may the next generation find a few who will die trying!

Thane Ury, OMS Missionary Scholar in Residence
Asbury University, Wilmore, KY

OMS Tributes

OMS India

Loving greetings in Christ. Glenda and I thank God for Wesley Duewel! What a privilege to know him and learn from him. Please be assured of our prayers for you all during this time of loss. Unfortunately, we will not be present for the celebration service. We are traveling to New Zealand today and will visit Glenda's 87-year-old mom and family living there. Nevertheless, our thoughts and prayers are with you. Hilda, we are so thankful for you and your loving devotion to Dr. Duewel. May the Lord comfort you and fill you with the peace of His presence. The life of Wesley Duewel was so unique and blessed by God. His example of love for Jesus and prayer will endure for generations to come. His impact upon the Kingdom of Christ will be fully revealed when the eternal day shines bright for us all and Christ reigns over consummated history. On behalf of my family as well as the family of OMS India ministries, we remember and celebrate the faithful life of Christ's servant Wesley Duewel. All praise be to God. Sincerely yours.

Roger and **Glenda Kruse**, OMS India Field Director
Middlefield, OH

OMS Tributes

Upon receiving the news of Dr. Duewel's passing, we were so very sad, yet we are confident that there is a magnificent and wonderful time of celebration in Heaven. He was certainly an inspiration to me as I ventured on to Indian soil and knowing he was praying for me was very encouraging. He will be greatly missed on many levels and things just won't be the same, but he has left us a faithful legacy to walk in the same shoes that he walked in. To daily trust God for the impossible. Much blessings to you all, as you farewell this faithful servant and hero of the Cross.

Chunilal Pema, former OMS India Missionary
OMS New Zealand

International Support Ministries

Dr. Duewel was a dear friend. Many times when I had guests visiting OMS I would take them over to meet him. He brought the funeral message for both of Peggy's parents and those services were in Southern Illinois. No OMS person has been known worldwide like Dr. Duewel.
It was my special privilege to go with him to Texas where he was awarded *Missio Nexus*' first ever Lifetime of Service Award. I cannot imagine the welcome he received and to think of his being with Jesus, whom he loved so dearly and served so diligently here on earth. His influence and impact is worldwide.

Donald and **Peggy Saum**, Director
International Support Ministries, Greenwood, IN

Men for Missions International

Remembering Dr. Wesley Duewel

Spiritually, Wesley Duewel was a giant of a man. He really lived *"All for Jesus."*

Two of my greatest honors in life have been to be asked by Dr. Duewel to assist him in healing services. He always stressed that there was nothing of man in healing. It was and is all about Jesus.

Then, to be privileged to be a member of the Duewel Literature Trust has been another honor. How blessed we are to have sat with Dr. Duewel, as he talked about 2.5 million books in 58 languages.

*Many, O Lord my God, are the wonders which you have done, and your thoughts toward us. (*Psalm 40:5)

Warren Hardig, Chairman, *Duewel Literature Trust*
Executive Director, *Men for Missions International*
Greenwood, IN

OMS Tributes

OMS New Zealand

We express our deepest condolences to you and your family for the departure of Dr. Wesley Duewel. He is and will continue to be one of my heroes and role models of the faith. We pray every comfort and blessing to the entire extended family.

Owen Brown, Executive Director
OMS New Zealand

OMS South Africa

As you may or may not be aware, my family had a long and special bond with Dr. Duewel over the years. He has always stayed with my grandparents and later with my parents during his various visits to South Africa. Since we will not be attending his memorial service, please kindly convey our condolences and love to his family. Dr. Duewel was most probably the godliest man I have ever met. He is safely home!! Love from Elda and me.

Warmly In Him,
Dawie Crous, Chairman of the Board
OMS South Africa

OMS Tributes

OMS Taiwan

I have always appreciated Dr. Duewel's consistent example of faith, passion, and humility.

Karen Neff, OMS Taiwan Missionary
Taichung, Taiwan

OMS United Kingdom

We in the United Kingdom appreciated all the leadership and challenge that Dr. Duewel exposed us to over his many visits. It was a tremendous privilege to have known Wesley and to have shared so many experiences and chats with him during his visits to our countries and to sit in the meetings he conducted in various centers.

His initial vision for the growth of churches in India got many supporters of OMS fired up to pray for the goal set of 1,000 churches. When this was achieved we continued to pray for the next 1,000.

Two memories stand out of his times here. He spoke at a large Christian conference in Bangor, County Down on prayer. He had recently published *Touch the World through Prayer*. So many came to hear Wesley that the church could not hold the people and several nearby halls had to be used and for some it was standing room only.

The second occasion was a few years later when he was researching for his book on *Revival Fire*. He was absolutely thrilled to be able to visit some of the sites of the 1859 Revival in Ulster as well as going to Slemish Mountain where the patron saint of Ireland, St. Patrick, had tended sheep as a young man before God used him to spread the gospel in Ireland.

Dr. Duewel's legacy to One Mission Society has been a network of prayer groups meeting in homes here especially in Northern Ireland, working out in practice the theme of his several books on the importance and effectiveness of prayer.

For those of us who were able to visit Greenwood it was a special privilege to be able to sit down with Wesley and be enthused by his passion for prayer and his interest in our own ministry. God alone knows the impact he has had on many believers in the United Kingdom and Ireland and we join with others all over the world in giving thanks for the blessings received through God's hand on Dr. Duewel in his ministry in public speaking, personal contact and inspirational writing.

Bill Burnett, Member Care Volunteer
OMS United Kingdom

OMS USA Finance Department

I've only been at OMS for about two years and he has already had such an influence on me. Dr. Duewel was such a prayer warrior—I'll never forget when he prayed at one of our chapel services—such an example.

Robyn Roller, OMS Assistant Treasurer
OMS Finance Department, Greenwood, IN

OMS Tributes

OMS Adult Missionary Children

We have just heard that Wesley passed away last month and we wanted to pass on our love and prayers to you and the family.

Uncle Wesley, as I used to call him, was certainly a great warrior for the Lord and has continued in ministry long after most other people have retired. I still recall his distinctive preaching style and his poetry. He was an inspiration and blessing to many.

It is quite a while since we saw him last, which was when he was out here in Australia. I had communicated a few times over the years and had also set up some phone calls with my parents before they both passed away.

Could you also please pass on our greetings (myself and my brother Colin) to the family? We all spent time together at Allahabad Bible Seminary when we were kids and my parents (Wal and Eunice Anderson) were working with Wesley and Betty. We also pray that you will know the presence of the Holy Spirit as comforter and friend in a very real way. God bless you.

Alan and **Peggy Anderson**, OMS India MK
Sydney, Australia

Thank you so much for sending on this message. I had so much admiration for Dr. Wesley Duewel. What a man of God! Always an inspiration wherever he went. Condolences and blessings to the family.

Mrs. **Christine** (Cavit) **Magee**, OMS Ecuador MK
Rochester, NY and Cuenca, Ecuador

OMS Tributes

OMS Missionary Retirees

My sister Evelyn and I traveled to the OMS office in Belfast, Northern Ireland to meet Dr. Duewel in the fall of 1964. I had applied to OMS but wasn't accepted yet. My acceptance came very soon after that.

We were so impressed by all that Dr. Duewel shared about his work in India! It was a most inspiring conversation! I left that office more determined than ever to serve the Lord with my whole heart and my sister the same. Over the years, we've thought of Dr. Duewel as a very dear friend who would take time to type a letter on a train! He was a great friendship builder and will be missed. But we all learned from him.

He ordained Bruce to the ministry and one of Bruce's desires was to attend his funeral, but because of his illness Bruce could not do it.

Bruce and **Mabel Callender**, OMS Mozambique Field Director
OMS Ecuador Field Director
Chicago, IL

In the card that Wesley sent to my mother and me when my father passed away, he wrote, *'Your loved one is more alive now than ever.'* These words gave us more comfort than anything else.

Sylvia (Knapp) **Ellis**, OMS Taiwan Missionary
Pensacola, Florida

OMS Tributes

Memories of "Uncle Wesley"

Wesley Duewel may be the only missionary who ever applied to an OMS field in which they had no work. It was 1940 and the field was India. The curious story of his call has been repeated so often that it has passed into mission lore. But for future generations, it bears repeating.

From earliest childhood, Wesley was endowed with prodigious interest in spiritual matters. His father, originally a Methodist pastor, was a preacher, Bible school president, and a leading light in the Fire Baptized Holiness Church. His mother, a devout woman of prayer, was for many years bedridden and painfully sensitive to both light and noise. This required a difficult environment for a small child. Through his early schooling and into high school, Wesley was so obviously intent on spiritual matters he earned the moniker "*The Little Minister*." This, in time he admits, became a painful label for a young teenager eager for peer approval.

At age five, on that unforgettable day, Wesley was playing with his toy cars in the sandbox. Whether it came accompanied by mystic light, an inner impression, he still is not quite sure. In any case, the call was so certain, so undeniable that even at that tender age, he had absolutely no doubt that it had a divine source. "*Wesley,*" the voice said, "*I want you to be a missionary and I want you to go to India*." Wesley immediately dropped his toys and dashed into the house, shouting, "*Mommy, Mommy, I must go to India. God has called me to India*." And then doubtless pondering the prospect of traveling to the other side of the globe alone, he added, "*And Mommy, I want you to go with me*!"

Wesley's father had been receiving the magazine *God's Revivalist*, issued by a small Bible school in Cincinnati, Ohio. The content seemed preoccupied by so-called holiness teachings, and no issue ever failed to include several articles by such renowned holiness preachers as Henry Morrison, Uncle Buddy Robinson, A.M. Hills, even Oswald Chambers. All reiterated the doctrine and personal experience of being filled with the Holy Spirit — sanctification, as it was commonly called.

These plain and powerful articles explained in fiery language the nature and necessity and means of the experience. For fire-baptized folk, like the Duewels, *God's Revivalist* was "*manna from heaven*." Without question, the family decided God's Bible School was to be Wesley's destiny for further schooling.

Wesley did not testify to the experience of sanctification when he arrived on the campus of God's Bible School (GBS). After a relatively brief time, under the fervent preaching of this doctrine, he began a quest for his own "*personal Pentecost*," as it was then called.

It is a fact that at this time holiness meetings at GBS were marked by happy clamor so hilarious, in fact, that GBS neighbors went to court to sue the school for disturbing the peace.

One evening that first term, Wesley under the weight of great conviction made his way to a dormitory window, looked out over the city, and appealed to God for the baptism. Then, at that very moment, an experience which he never forgot occurred. It convinced him that he was indeed filled with the Spirit and empowered to not only win the lost but also to lead them into the doctrine of which John spoke when he said, "*There comes one after me who will baptize you with fire and the Holy Spirit*." Thereafter, he never doubted the experience and never ceased to preach that precious doctrine with a shining countenance.

Shortly after, Wesley met Betty Raisch. They fell in love and commenced their courtship. Betty was not only devout and extremely attractive but also an outstanding scholar who graduated as class salutatorian, a year behind Wesley who was valedictorian.

Since close association with the opposite sex on campus was frowned on, even forbidden, Wesley and Betty devised an ingenious scheme to further their courtship. Betty got a job in the college library, and Wesley found a position as assistant professor. This made both of them technically members of the college staff. As such they were not subject to the usual restrictions regarding the mingling of sexes. This arrangement soon became obvious to both students and faculty. None, however, felt in any way the necessity of impeding these two young people who so obviously loved the Lord with all their hearts and were, indeed, planning to serve Him as missionaries in India.

During his senior year at GBS, Wesley met Eugene Erny, a young missionary with The Oriental Missionary Society whose wife, Esther Helsby, and her parents had all attended GBS.

In late 1938 or early 1939, while Eugene was on the GBS campus, Wesley took him aside and asked if OMS was going to open work in India? He had, in fact, already made preliminary application but had been informed that OMS, at that time, had no plans to open a field in India. Still Wesley explained, God had called him to India. What could be done?

Great War clouds were gathering on the horizon and threatening OMS fields in Japan, Korea and China. Eugene knew that recently the mission board had, indeed, been giving serious thought to opening work in India, still relatively tranquil as a British colony. His response to Wesley was,

OMS Tributes

"We presently have no work in India but I know the board is considering it. You pray about it and we'll pray also."

Two years later, in 1941 OMS commenced work in India. Eugene had been marked for the field leader, and first applicants were the Duewels and Seamands. Earlier in 1930 when Eugene, Byron Crouse and Virgil Kirkpatrick had toured the world on their famous Asbury College mission campaign, their journeys took them to India. Here, Eugene wrote in his diary that he felt a very strong impression that at some time God would lead him to India. Now that call was about to be fulfilled.

The OMS team all arrived in south India to rendezvous at the home of Methodist pioneer E.A. Seamands, whose sons, J.T. and David, were students at Asbury College, Eugene's alma mater. At this time of the well-entrenched British Raj, some missionaries were influenced by the social habits of the military families. Upon arrival, Mrs. Seamands took the OMS ladies aside to instruct them to waste no time in buying evening gowns for social occasions to which they were sure to be invited. (Somehow Eugene and Wesley did not feel that this kind of purchase could be easily accommodated within the OMS faith mission world view.) After a brief stay with the elder Seamands, the OMS team located in Bangalore, a beautiful southern city. There they lived together in a large newly-constructed bungalow as one happy family. These were halcyon days for all except Bobby and Edward Erny who had no choice but to go to an Anglo-Indian school, notorious for corporeal punishment which was practiced on a daily basis.

Most of that year the team members conducted an investigation into the social, linguistic and culture conditions best suited for an OMS mission site. They finally chose a large city in the north, Allahabad. Originally a famous Muslim center, it was named Allahabad, "the abode of Allah."

The other station was a small city in southern India, a Kanarese-speaking center called Gadag.

Our family was situated on the OMS compound in Allahabad where the Duewels were our neighbors. Wesley, we soon learned, was perhaps the most devout, passionate missionary one could ever meet. Curiously, he was also the perfect uncle. He played lively songs on a banjo and joined in the popular table games, Sorry and Parcheesi. He also had a great sense of humor and, when aroused, dissolved into paroxysms of laughter. He had a rich repertoire of funny anecdotes, some stemming from his Bible school days. One story I recall today, 60 years later, was a prank during the great flood. At this time much of the city of Cincinnati was under water and this had fostered a considerable increase in the population of frogs. One imaginative dorm mate caught a number of the lively creatures, put them in a box which he secretly fastened directly above his roommate's bed. That night, when it was dark, he quizzed his roommate on the plagues of Egypt. He wondered if he could recite them all. His roommate thoughtfully recalled the flies, the great darkness, the lice and then the plague of frogs. At this precise moment, the prankster pulled a nearly invisible thread, opening the box and dumping its contents. Just as the scholar announced the plague of the frogs, he felt something, in fact many things dark and wet falling on his face. A terrible silence followed and then a guttural scream, "Frogs, frogs, I have frogs all over me." In reciting this anecdote, Wesley was all but consumed by waves of risibility.

When the Duewels arrived in India, they were in their early 20s. Wesley's slender physique and mild, gentle manner gave him the appearance of a much younger man, possibly even a teenager. This, he soon learned, was not an asset in so serious a line of work as a minister or seminary professor. Shortly thereafter, it was noted that he had allowed some slight foliage to appear on his upper lip. Growing and thriving, it took the appearance of a respectable moustache, unfortunately quite like Charlie Chaplin's, a popular film star of the time.

For us, childhood anecdotes involving Wesley and Betty Duewel increased in number with every vacation which we spent in Allahabad, just across the way from the Duewel bungalow.

Most memorable was the year we returned home as usual in late November from boarding school for winter vacation. So excited were we to be back on the grand, old compound, Bob and I could not sleep. We wakened at about 4 a.m. We knew, of course, that rising at that hour would not be a popular move. Still, we were so happily agitated that we could not remain in bed. We decided to cautiously creep up the side stairs to the broad, flat house top. All the compound roofs were inter-connected, enabling us to traverse virtually the entire compound by roof, from the school dormitories to missionary residences. Climbing the wall from the boys' dorm to the adjacent Duewel bungalow was far more of a feat than we had imagined. In the pitch darkness, we groped our way across the elevated archways and began a careful assent up the side of the building to the Duewels' veranda. Placing our toes in the square notches on the side of the building was the only way to achieve this difficult assent. So we began, Bob first and I behind. This was a considerable maneuver to say the least and impossible to achieve without loud whispers, communications, grunts, and hoarse half-muffled cries of caution.

As we finally reached the top and began to straddle the veranda banister, a dark, trembling figure appeared out of nowhere, brandishing a huge club (we later discovered it was a baseball bat), threatening our demise. Suddenly the man halted in his mischievous course. He had equipped himself with a flashlight. By the soft shaft of light, he discovered that the miscreants were not burglars at all but the Erny boys. Of all our playful endeavors during those ten years of vacation time on the OMS campus, this is the one Wesley remembers best and repeats with fresh zeal to anyone who will listen.

To appreciate how much of a prankster Wesley was I need to recount what was surely his favorite trick. At the annual student party, Wesley would have all the students stand about in a circle. Then a student and a faculty member (usually Wesley himself) were instructed to lie on the floor in the middle of the circle, their heads covered with a blanket. The students were furnished a club fashioned from a long, rather hard, roll of cardboard. The club, the prone victims were informed, would be passed from student to student around the circle and periodically one of them would use it with fervor on their backsides. The victims then were to uncover their heads and determine who it was that had struck them. Their efforts were frustrated again and again. In the end it was finally revealed that the violence was not the work of one of the students at all but Wesley, lying adjacent to his hapless partner, was periodically thrashing him and then quickly replacing the club under the blanket. It was as hilarious a trick as I have ever seen. . . .

This is but a brief recollection of memorable associations with the Duewels during the last 50 years. The full disclosure will have to await the publication of Wesley's memoirs in the hopefully near future.

Edward Erny, OMS President, OMS Philippines Field Missionary
OMS Taiwan Field Missionary, OMS India MK
Greenwood, IN

OMS Tributes

Remembering Wesley Duewel

Wesley took over the editing of Revival Magazine from my Dad in India. He contributed many articles to that magazine. Perhaps the mission has copies in its archives. I believe Wesley's passion has always been revival and prayer. Much of his writing has been on these subjects. While Wesley did teach theology in Allahabad, I do not think of him as a theologian or academician. He did prepare a statement on the gifts of the Spirit, specifically addressing the matter of tongues, for the OMS Bylaws, which I felt was well balanced. He also wrote a theological textbook (*God's Great Salvation*) for use of village pastors, formulating clearly our Wesleyan doctrines of entire sanctification, holiness, etc. I feel OMS and the wider world will best remember Wesley for his passion for prayer and revival, as expressed in his writing and preaching.

Robert Erny, VP of OMS-USA, VP of Field Ministries, OMS Hong Kong Field Director, OMS Indonesia Field Director, OMS India MK
Wilmore, KY

What a God-filled legacy he has left to OMS and the Bruce Hess family in particular. Wesley's example of prayer and depth of teaching and discipleship will ever be part of our DNA. God be praised forever.

Bruce and **Donna Hess**, OMS USA Regional Director
OMS Colombia Field Missionary
Houghton, NY

I personally have many fond memories of serving with him, not only here in the States but in Russia as well. He jokingly said to me once that I could probably give his prayer seminar as well as he could. I had been with him that many times.

He will be missed but we rejoice in his faithful ministry in challenging and writing about his journey of faith. We will all be praying for Hilda and the other members of the family.

Blessings,
Austin Sullivan, Associate OMS Regional Director, OMS Russia CoMission
Allentown, PA

Words cannot express our caring for Wesley. Howard and I have been with him in conventions, etc. And his burning desire to challenge us all to pray and care.

Bless his memory.
Mrs. **Wilma Jacob**, OMS Regional Director
Port Orange, Florida

We remember fondly when we first met Dr. Duewel. We participated in a college and career weekend and stayed at his and Betty's home. We were in awe because he was OMS' president. When we walked in, he said, '*I knew God was going to teach me something new this weekend! I always wanted to know the first name of Noah's wife*!' We felt at ease immediately.

Another time, he stayed in our home in Brazil. He was walking down the hallway to his room when he turned to me and said, '*You know, my mother did give me a first name*.' We always addressed him as '*Dr. Duewel*.' We laughed, but still addressed him as '*Dr. Duewel*.' '*Wesley*' seemed to stick in my throat. We appreciated him so much and praise God for the tremendous legacy of holy living and prayer he left.

Psalm 116:15
Mel and **Fran Noah**, OMS Brazil Field Director
Wilmore, KY

OMS Tributes

I shall always be grateful and have been blessed by my high privilege of being a colleague of Wesley's in India! He was a loyal supporter in prayer and encouragement as Eleanore and I went through very hard experiences in India. Thank God for his understanding and help at that time. Many know this and have said it (far better than I could) that Wesley was truly a man of God whose life and service for Jesus will bear eternal dividends! Thanks to you, Hilda, for all of your loving contributions by helping him to complete his race so triumphantly!"

Rudolph Rabe, OMS India Missionary Coworker
Tucson, AZ

Remembering Dr. Wesley Duewel

It is an honor for me to share how Dr. Wesley Duewel has blessed my life. His example, his teaching, his leadership and his writing have all been of benefit to me.

First, what I remember of his public life. Seeing Wesley and Betty at the OMS conferences (early 1960's) dressed in their native Indian costumes was impressive. Listening to Wesley relate the physical and spiritual challenges of ministry in India made me realize here was a true missionary and servant of the Lord.

I was impressed that Wesley was a "doctor" with an earned D.Ed. perhaps the only one in OMS at that time. Certainly this was an added asset for sharing the Gospel and training church workers in India. This was an example of the importance of proper preparation before going to the mission field.

OMS Tributes

When Dr. Erny retired from the presidency of OMS the board must have recognized that Dr. Duewel had the qualifications to fill that role with distinction. He certainly could preach with passion both the message of missions and its counterpart, the life of holiness. Wesley prepared his messages well, and took as much time as he needed to preach, even though at times it seemed long to some of us.

Dr. Duewel had his own method of preparing his class notes for teaching at the seminary. And he was happy to share his notes when requested. I benefited from those notes in my own preparation for teaching in Taiwan. The notes reveal careful exegesis, logical development and with full and complete coverage of the subject; a style that is seen also in his later publications. I never read the *Revival Magazine* that he published in India, but what a valuable extension of his preaching and teaching that must have been.

As a young missionary I appreciated his leadership and viewed it as successful. I am sure he faced administrative challenges with which only he and his leadership team had to cope. Later, as a field leader, I was privileged to attend board meetings and observed how he shared his vision and passion for all of the expanding ministries of OMS. He was willing to take steps of faith for new outreach, yet wanting to know the Lord's will and direction.

I was also impressed that inter-mission agencies, like EFMA, at that time also recognized Dr. Duewel's expertise and elected him to its leadership, expanding his influence even further.

Retirement from OMS certainly did not decrease his public ministries, but gave him more time to concentrate on writing and sharing in leading spiritual life and prayer retreats, but still faithful to uphold all the OMS work. When I was privileged to attend OMS chapel, I always appreciated hearing Dr. Duewel pray. He always seemed to reach right into the Lord's presence.

Dr. Duewel's personal life was even more of an example to me of a true follower of Jesus Christ. As a young missionary we called our senior missionaries Aunt and Uncle so-and-so, but never Dr. Duewel. It only seemed proper to show him the respect due him and his position. OMS MKs in India may have called him *"Uncle Wesley."* Of course, now it is easy just to address him as Wesley, but with no less respect.

I never tired hearing Wesley relate his call to missions and how he was so clearly led into OMS and to India. That was inspiring. And he always had a good "missionary" story to relate that proved the Lord's faithfulness, inspiring us to also trust the Lord more fully. His life and work of laying the foundations of OMS work in India stands as a model for all of us.

Obviously, the OMS president could not visit all the fields frequently, but when he could come we wanted him to minister to us and also to our national coworkers. He had so much he could share, and knew what we needed as well. So he always had a full schedule of meetings, but also took time to visit individually. He had genuine concern for our personal needs and we knew he would be faithful in praying for us as well.

On one such visit, it was stormy, a real typhoon hit us. Dr. Duewel seemed excited to be able to witness such a storm. He ran from window to window to get a better view of what the wind was doing.

One amusing incident we will always remember. It was an evening of fellowship with the mission family in Taiwan. Doug and Judy Carr from Australia were on the field and came with their newborn daughter to the gathering. We discovered that Aussie terms often differ from ours. Judy took the baby to Dr. Duewel and asked, "*Would you like to nurse Sarah*"? Without a moment's hesitation, Dr. Duewel replied, "*Well, I do believe in a God of miracles*!" And he enjoyed a few moments cuddling the baby.

Dr. Duewel was real. A real human, yet humble, honoring the Lord with all his many gifts, so we benefited from his leadership, preaching, teaching, writing, and especially his praying. A faithful dedicated servant of his Savior and Lord, one who wanted his Lord to get all the glory.

Lowell Williamson, OMS Asia-Pacific Regional Director
OMS Taiwan Field Director
Wilmore, KY

It is Well with My Soul

When peace like a river attendeth my way,
When sorrows like sea billows roll,
Whatever my lot, Thou hast taught me to say,
"It is well, it is well with my soul."

Refrain: (4x)
It is well with my soul; it is well,
It is well with my soul!

Though Satan should buffet, though trials should come,
Let this blest assurance control,
That Christ hath regarded my helpless estate,
And hath shed His own blood for my soul.

My sin–oh, the bliss of this glorious thought–
My sin, not in part but the whole,
Is nailed to His cross and I bear it no more!
Praise the Lord, praise the Lord, O my soul!

And, Lord, haste the day when the faith shall be sight,
The clouds be rolled back as a scroll,
The trump shall resound, and the Lord shall descend!
Even so–it is well with my soul!

Horatio G. Stafford 1828–1888
Mid-Atlantic, 1873

Organizational and Individual Tributes

Introduction to the Organizational and Individual Tributes

The following ministries and leaders offered tributes and testimonials because of the positive and long lasting influence Dr. Duewel had on them organizationally or personally. His writings were frequently, if not regularly, reprinted in the respective organizational publications, and in many instances his counsel was sought during the launching of particular ministries. The prayer partner tributes and testimonies included herein only serve to symbolize many more who have been positively impacted by Dr. Duewel's lifelong habit of intercessory prayer, public preaching and publications, as well as the private and personal counsel shared with so many.

Asian Outreach

We are sorry to hear of the passing away of our dear Dr. Duewel. May this Celebration of Life be a time of comfort to you and a reminder of prayer and world mission to the participants and those paying their respects. We deeply appreciate your passion for the church in China. It is surely the most potential mission force of the 21st Century.

I had the opportunity to be present at one of the distributions of Dr. Duewel's three books in a seminary. We taught five days on missions, and then distributed a set of these books to each of the participants, so that they could learn how to engage in missions through prayer. Even though we know that the students come from different churches of various sizes, the local teacher in charge was so careful that the students who want more copies for their church leaders, have to talk to her in person one by one, so that no copies would be wasted.

We are thankful that we can partner together for the expansion of His Kingdom. As China opens up more and more, and building friendship with her neighboring countries, we see opportunities for China's Christians to be involved in prayer and in actual mission going. The demand for these books would continue and increasing so.

Best regards,
James Chak, General Director
Asian Outreach, Hong Kong

Christian Renewal Ministries

Our dear friend and prayer partner—what a man of God so mightily used to touch the lives of millions! How blessed I was to know him and pray with him. Oh, how God used him to help me and my ministry!

James and **Shirley Tharp**, President
Christian Renewal Ministries, Bozeman, MT

CLC Publications

Thank you for informing me of this news, I am so sorry for your loss and will be praying for you and your family. I have to say that it is an amazing testimony and encouragement to me, someone who has been married for less than 2 years, to see a couple together until the age of 99. Thank you for being an example to the next generation of married couples. May God bless your faithfulness and give you peace during this time.

Sincerely,
Scott Endicott, Sales Coordinator
CLC Publications, Ft. Washington, PA

Community Owners Business Alliance

The Quiet Passing of a Christian Evangelist, Leader, Author, and Faithful Intercessor

Dr. Wesley L. Duewel was born in St. Charles, Missouri, in 1916, to Christian parents, his father being an evangelical pastor. Wesley and his late wife Betty ministered in India, as the Oriental Missionary Society (now One Mission Society) evangelism missionaries for 25 years. After his return from India, Dr. Duewel led OMS as its president. Upon stepping down from those heady responsibilities, Wesley turned his attention to writing and poetry. Several of his dozen books, in the minds of many Christian readers, have become classics – on the subjects of prayer and evangelism. To date, there are more than "...2.5 million in circulation, printed in 58 languages." (See also *'Living a Legacy'* biography in a recent OMS periodical.) Wesley is frequently quoted by many authors in their books.

On a personal note, I've long considered Wesley, and his wife Hilda, to be genuine and faithful friends. My sole concern, in bringing his passing to your attention, is it's rare to enjoy such a unique individual in one's local society, who over a period of 99 years, has served God as a Christian evangelist, been a leader of his peers, the author of many popular books; and though generally not known, one who has been passionate in personal petition praying, and faithfully interceding in behalf of acquaintances, family members, and friends around the world! Many will miss Dr. Wesley L. Duewel.

Organizational and Individual Tributes

What I share here is not an elegy, an epitaph, or eulogy, for our friend and fellow intercessor, Wesley Duewel; but a valediction – 'a fond farewell' till we meet again in God's presence. For as is oft said, and I truly believe, 'Those who love God, *and embrace Jesus Christ as Savior*, never meet for the last time!'

Now, talk about someone whose life has truly spanned the ages, Wesley Duewel, born in St. Charles, Missouri, during leap year 1916, certainly did!

World War I, was in its' third of four years duration at the time, the PGA was birthed in New York City that year, U.S. Marines invaded the Dominican Republic, and a first-class stamp cost (Gasp!) only 2 cents!

'Spiffy' terms used by college students in 1916, were: 'brick' and 'peach', as 'terms of approval' for men and women respectively; a 'sluffer' didn't take life seriously, and 'spoofing' was (and still is) banter or making fun.

Now, fast forward 99 years to 2016! Following 25 years as a missionary to India, and nearly 75 years of service to the One Mission Society family, Wesley has 100+ entries on google! Now, that's 'spanning the ages'!

Everyone has their special Wesley Duewel book and favorite quotations. Mine? *God's Power is For You,* 1997. I've read it cover to cover nine times!

My favorite passages? His stirring firsthand description, in the 'Winds of Revival' chapter, of Holy Spirit revival during a chapel service at Asbury College on 3 February 1970 - a revival that lasted for months afterward!

And one of several favorite personal quotes is found on page 111. I've long felt Wesley penned these words for me: *"May God use these brief meditations again and again to add burning coals to your soul's altar and cause you to blaze for Him. You are important to God."*

In 2003 I shared with Wesley, how one could use the first letter of six words in the following sentence, to create the acronym P R A Y E R: 'Prayer Really Affects Your Everyday Relationship with God!' Wesley responded, in a letter back to me, suggesting addition of "...and others!"

For me, there's only one way to conclude this valediction, this 'fond farewell' to Wesley Duewel; and it's with the reading of one of his many poems. This one, titled, *'Invest Your Life for God,'* is quoted from *Measure Your Life,* Zondervan, 1992.

Invest your time for eternity;
Invest your life for the life to be
Forever gone are the hours you've lost.
Don't waste your life; count again the cost.

Your money placed in the Savior's hand;
It's only safe when on heaven's strand.
You never lose what you give to God,
But lose all else when beneath the sod.

Invest your work in the Savior's plan;
Work hard for God and His will for man.
Don't count the hours you toil and plod –
You'll reap again all you do for God.

Don't waste your life for a passing joy;
Don't sell your soul for a fragile toy.
Give till it hurts; give your very blood –
You live but once; live all out for God.

So, 'fond farewell' – for now, Wesley, till we meet again in God's presence!

George Allen, Author and Freelance Consultant
Greenwood, IN

Free Methodist Church

It was an eventful day in 1966 when Wesley Duewel came to my late husband's (Don Riggs) office at the West Morris Street Free Methodist Church in Indianapolis, Indiana. A phone call was placed to inform Bishop Paul Ellis at the Free Methodist World Ministries Center that Dr. Duewel was interested in transferring his ministerial credentials to the Free Methodist denomination. Bishop Ellis immediately met Wesley Duewel and Pastor Don Riggs at the church and a half-century partnership followed.

Often Dr. Duewel would return from an overseas trip just the day before, or even early on the Sabbath morning, but he would be at the church to teach the Sanctuary Sunday School Class for the majority of fifty years. In those early years, his wife, Betty, and his youngest daughter, Darlene, were by his side. Darlene was a faithful participant in the youth group and the teen choir, The SPARCS.

Over the years we have been privileged and enjoyed hosting several of the Duewel family in our home. When looking through a file of the Duewel family kept by Don, I found numerous photos, personal letters, notes, and programs, workshop outlines of events, newspaper articles, prayer letters, numerous prayer inventories, and articles about the Duewels. Among the programs was the memorial service for dear Betty. There was also the Christmas letter announcing the marriage of Hilda Johnecheck and Wesley; both events were officiated by Don Riggs.

Dr. Duewel's counsel and friendship has been a treasured blessing to our family, and certainly his leadership, dedicated partnership, and participation in the Free Methodist denomination is highly respected.

Reverently and Respectfully,
Mrs. Don (**Iris**) **Riggs**, wife of former senior pastor
West Morris Street Free Methodist Church, Indianapolis, IN

Mrs. Iris and Dr. Donald Riggs who officiated at Wesley and Hilda's wedding

Organizational and Individual Tributes

After 75 years of missionary service with OMS and 48 years of ordained ministry in Wabash Conference of the Free Methodist Church, last July at the 131st annual meeting of Wabash Conference, Wesley Duewel officially retired from itinerant ministry at the age of 99. That was a record. Years ago Wesley told me that God gave him a promise from Psalm 91:16: *"With long life will I satisfy him and show him my salvation."* Wesley humbly embraced that promise and maintained a very long view of life that splashed over into eternity. It wasn't just longevity that characterized Wesley's life and ministry...it was his faithful, disciplined, and effective use of the time and the gifts that God gave him that made his life so impactful on a world stage. Eugene Peterson once described Christian discipleship as *"A long obedience in the same direction."* That was Wesley Duewel's life.

He taught a Sunday School class in this church for 46 years. Through the years he often spent from 2 to 3 hours in prayer daily. His 25-year investment in mission work in India laid the foundation for a movement of God that today includes over 16,000 churches and 13 Bible Schools and Seminaries. He read through the Old Testament 209 times, and the New Testament 354 times. Yes, he actually kept track. He was a Wesleyan Methodist through and through! He wrote ten major books including *Touch the World through Prayer*, *Ablaze for God*, and *Revival Fire*. There are over 2.5 million copies of his books in print and his works have been translated into 58 languages. He was a scholar, a poet (he composed nearly 1,000), a pastor, a missionary, a friend, and a faithful husband and father whose life purpose was to reflect the heart, character, and mission of God.

This church, and the Free Methodist Church family as a whole, have been so blessed by the presence, example, and the ministry of this World Class follower of Jesus, whose life of service to the Lord has impacted so many people here and around the world. Thank you, Wesley, for leaving us such a powerful example of what it means to follow Jesus.

Mike Conkle, Former Senior Pastor
West Morris Street Free Methodist Church, Indianapolis, IN

The greatest blessing, or at least one of them, is the privilege we had of knowing Dr. Duewel, listening to his wisdom, observing his dedication to God.

Steve and **Judy Strange**
West Morris Street Free Methodist Church, Adult Education
Avon, IN

Gospel Revivals, Inc.

The Celebration of Life service was a precious time in honoring our dear brother Wesley whose life and ministry brought such honor and glory to the Lord. Gayla, Gail and I were blessed to be there, but we were not there in time to make it through the line beforehand to greet you. The whole service was very meaningful and we were blessed by all who participated in it. We also appreciated how Wesley's heart for the unsaved (and even more, the Lord's heart for the unsaved) was shared and that those in attendance had the opportunity to hear the Gospel message. We continue to pray for unsaved family to open their hearts to the Lord for salvation. We appreciate your sending the link to us for the service, and we will pass that on to others. I was also honored to join with other ministers in singing "*It Is Well with My Soul*." We are wondering about the status of our Brother Wesley's autobiography? Was he able to complete it? Will it become available? If so, we will be interested in obtaining several copies.

You continue to be much in our hearts and prayers. May the Lord pour out His comfort, strength and encouragement on you day by day. We thought it was beautiful the way others, including Wesley's children, expressed their appreciation for the wonderful love and care you provided to Wesley. You certainly are a gift, not only to Wesley and his family, but to many others, including all of the grace you have shown toward the Herald ministry and staff. We appreciate you very much. To God be the glory!

In His love,
Rich Carmicheal, Director
Gospel Revivals Inc., Seelyville, IN

Hagnos Publishing

I heard that Dr. Duewel passed away, I am sorry to know that, but of course now he is in God's wonderful presence. I just want to let you know that we pray that God give you comfort and peace to your heart. And Dr. Duewel's books will continue to talk to the Brazilian's heart.

May God be with you,
Marilene Terrengui, President
Hagnos Publishing, Sao Paulo, Brazil

Thank you for your information and we are praying for God to console your heart. We will try to watch this live stream transmission tomorrow.

God bless you,
Juan Martinez, Editor
Hagnos Publishing, Sao Paulo, Brazil

Organizational and Individual Tributes

Herald of His Coming

Our dear brother Wesley L. Duewel went home to be with the Lord on March 5, 2016, at the age of 99. Throughout his life he was devoted to world missions, serving 25 years as a missionary to India, and then as president of One Mission Society. He was devoted to the Word of God and prayer, and he wrote ten books encouraging and challenging God's people in vital spiritual matters such as prayer, revival, soul winning and fullness of the Holy Spirit.

For many years he was a great blessing to Herald of His Coming, serving as an advisory board member and faithfully praying for the ministry and the staff. He also graciously allowed the Herald ministry to freely reprint from his writings. On page four in this issue we include "Be God's Miracle" by Brother Duewel, an article that we first printed in 1980. Though this is a rather brief article, it nevertheless provides a good example of the level of encouragement, challenge and inspiration contained in his writings.

Brother Sanu, the Herald's representative in Nigeria, had the opportunity in 2005 to spend time with Brother Duewel during a visit to the U.S. Upon hearing about Brother Duewel's death, Brother Sanu paid this fitting tribute to him: "*We bless the Name of the Lord for this General in God's army of intercessors. The Lord has taken His own after a meritorious service for a well-deserved rest. Indeed he has fought the good fight, he has kept the faith, and he has finished his course. Henceforth there is laid for him a crown of righteousness which the righteous God shall give to him, and not only to him, but to all who love His appearing.*" The Herald staff joins in blessing the Lord for this precious brother and dear servant.

To God be the Glory!

Rich Carmicheal, Editor
The Herald of His Coming, Seelyville, IN

Humboldt, Nebraska Hometown Newspaper

Tribute to Humboldt Native Wesley L. Duewel
(June 3, 1916 - March 5, 2016)

An interesting headline highlighted Page 4 of the May 2016 edition of *Herald of His Coming* magazine. It read, "Dr. Wesley L. Duewel—Home with the Lord." Who is Wesley Duewel, you ask?

Some eight or nine decades ago there lived in the town of Humboldt a quiet, humble woman named Ida Duewel. Though she was not all that noteworthy by most people's standards, there was one thing that set her apart—her fervency for prayer. It is said that she would spend two or three hours each day in prayer, crying out to God to touch the town of Humboldt. Did her prayers make any difference—in Humboldt, Nebraska—or anywhere else, for that matter?

They certainly impacted her son, and through him, millions around the world. In fact, Wesley, a graduate of Humboldt High School Class of 1935, went on to be an outstanding scholar, pulpiteer, missionary, and writer.

Probably none of Duewel's classmates could ever have imagined that Wesley's 10 books would have been printed in 58 languages, and reached 2.5 million people. It is a rare thing for a writer to receive word that his first major book fell into the hands of nearly a million avid readers.

But Wesley Duewel was no ordinary preacher, missionary, or writer. No, he was a man whose roots were in a little town in Nebraska; who inspired millions as he walked with God as His humble servant.

Those who knew Dr. Duewel found His emphasis on fervency in prayer and a personal experience with the power of the Holy Spirit to be the answer for frustrated defeated believers to become joyful overcomers.

I am so thankful that on Easter Sunday in 1978, I had the privilege of kneeling in prayer with that member of Humboldt High's class of 1935!

Prevailing in Prayer—Quotes by Dr. Wesley L. Duewel

THE GREAT NEED of our world, our nation, and our churches is people who know how to PREVAIL in PRAYER.

Moments of pious wishes blandly expressed to God once or twice a day will bring little change on earth or among the people. Kind thoughts expressed to Him in five or six sentences, after reading a paragraph or two of mildly religious sentiments once a day from some devotional writing, will not bring the kingdom of God to earth or shake the gates of hell and repel the attacks of evil on our culture and our civilization.

PREVAILING PRAYER is prayer that PUSHES right through all difficulties and obstacles, drives back all the opposing forces of Satan, and secures the will of God. Its purpose is to accomplish God's will on earth. Prevailing prayer is prayer that not only takes the initiative but continues on the offensive for God until spiritual victory is won.

Ronald and **Caroline Russell**, local minister
Humboldt, NE

Japan Holiness Church

May God give you comfort and the light of mercy from His graceful face. We want to express our appreciation for Dr. Wesley Duewel's servant-hood for the OMS family all over the world. We all remember that Dr. Duewel visited Japan and gave us encouraging messages at our 80th anniversary service. His books were translated into Japanese and have been a great blessing for the churches in Japan. We praise God for the fruit of Dr. Duewel's faithful work for the Lord. We believe that Dr. Duewel's vision, his faithful work for the Lord, and his prayers will continue to produce much fruit and will be a blessing in Japan and all over the world, even for the next generation. May our gracious Father God give His comfort upon all of you.

Sincerely,
Masahiro Nakanishi, Executive Committee, Japan Holiness Church
Higashimurayama Shi, Tokyo, Japan

Thank you so much for letting us know about Dr. Duewel. It is our privilege to have met with him when we were in Greenwood. We pray for God's comfort to his family.

Takanori Inoue, Japan Holiness Church
Asbury Theological Seminary, Lexington, KY

John 17 Ministries

"Ablaze For God! Your personality so suffused with the presence and beauty of the Lord that others instinctively sense that God is with you! God's hand so clearly evident upon your life and leadership that a quiet holy power and authority seem to rest upon you!"

Organizational and Individual Tributes

These words were penned by Dr. Wesley Duewel, a pioneer missionary to India and former President of OMS. However, to millions around the world, he was better known as a passionate lover of Jesus who lived to pray and to call others to live in His power. Dr. Duewel, age 99, joined the Cloud of Witnesses this year. To the very end, he kept the Spirit's fire, "lived" in the Throne room, and held a lost world lovingly in his heart.

As you read his words, I invite you to feel God's fire upon his life, and even more so, I invite you to catch fire! I also invite you to consider his words as a prayer guide to pray for you and your loved ones, your pastors and churches, and our J17 leaders and ministries here and abroad.

Susan Watson, Founder and Director
John 17 Ministries, Greenwood, IN

Missio Nexus

I remember reading Dr. Duewel's book on prayer as a young believer. It was influential in my life. It's so encouraging to know of a man who was faithful to the end of his life. 99 years – what a testimony. May the Lord bless his family and those who carry on his legacy.

Ted Esler, President
Missio Nexus (Originally the EFMA)*, Wheaton, IL*

First Recipient of "Lifetime of Service Award" Promoted to Glory

We celebrate the life of missionary statesman Wesley Duewel who, at 99 years of age, passed into glory. We so valued his contributions to the greater world of missions that in 2007 Dr. Duewel became the first recipient of the *Missio Nexus* annual prestigious *"Lifetime of Service*

Award." Among other outstanding achievements, he was president of OMS International for 13 years.

Whenever a long-revered missionary statesman – as Dr. Duewel undeniably was – is promoted to glory, there is much rejoicing! The many who have entered the Kingdom through his untiring missionary efforts rejoice. The many who have been mobilized and have given themselves to cross-cultural missionary service because of him, rejoice. The many who have been impacted by his faithful advocating of the primacy of the Great Commission rejoice. The many who under his wise leadership administered, managed and sat on various influential boards with him rejoice. The many who were profoundly impacted by his insightful books and writings rejoice. Indeed, even the angels in glory rejoice as they welcome the saint and statesman into his eternal home. We at *Missio Nexus* also rejoice. We rejoice in the influential life and global ministry of Wesley Duewel.

Marvin Newell, Senior Vice President
Missio Nexus (Originally the EFMA)*, Wheaton, IL*

New Beginning Church and West Africa Theological Seminary

It was a mere one hour ago that we very belatedly received information about the home going of Dr. Wesley Duewel last Saturday. Our hearts were saddened to know that at long last his voice and his pen have been irrevocably silenced here below. Yet at the same time, we realize that we have witnessed the passing of a true giant in our day and one who surely longed to be with the Jesus he so faithfully served.

Dr. Duewel had a very special place in the hearts of not just thousands, but certainly tens, if not hundreds of thousands of Nigerians. Since our first step in getting 10,000 copies of "*Touch the World through Prayer*" out into this country, we have seen the dissemination of hundreds of thousands of his books. We will never know the exact number, simply because eventually his books became popular enough that numerous unauthorized reprintings were made in various parts of the country. His books continue to be used as textbooks in Bible colleges around the country, as well as being widely distributed among churches.

Dr. Duewel's 1994 visit to Nigeria was a highlight for many of us, with national prayer conferences in eastern, northern and western Nigeria. There he spoke to many thousands and always with an inspiring message backed by a simple and godly life.

My personal interaction with Dr. Duewel on numerous visits to his office always left me with a very fresh respect for all God used him to do for the heavenly kingdom over the years. He always had timely counsel and was generous in supporting the interests of West Africa Theological Seminary.

We regret that because of the long distances we will not be able to be present for the funeral service next week. However, we assure you of our prayers and of our thanks to you for taking such loving care of our great hero over the past seven years. God bless you!

Sincerely,
Gary and **Emma Lou Maxey**, Founder
West Africa Theological Seminary (WATS) and Pastor of New Beginning Church, Lagos, Nigeria

Organizational and Individual Tributes

Operation Mobilization

Thank you so much for sharing this news. I heard this news and shared it with many Operation Mobilization leaders. Wesley and I have been linked since meeting in India around 1964. PTL! We extend our love and condolences.

In His grip,
George Verwer, Founder and former International Director
Operation Mobilization, United Kingdom

I am sorry for you loss. My parents (esp. my Father) and I are deeply saddened to know that Brother Wesley is no more with us. I can't write down how much he means to me. I am going miss him, too. I have been thinking and praying for him since 2004 or 2005, ever since I read his book. I met Brother K.C. Joseph (OM India Director), a sweet and wonderful man of God. He agreed to publish the book *"Let God Guide You Daily"* into Telugu after consulting with you.

With love and prayers,
Cephas JohnHyde Kolapudi
Operation Mobilization, Hyderabad, India

Prayer Partner Tributes

It is with great joy to know Dr. Duewel is with his India brothers and sisters and with Jesus; and yet also with great sadness because he was such a mentor of mine and Dawn's, and such an honor and pleasure to have worked alongside him.

Paul and **Dawn Cox**, former OMS missionaries
Houston, TX

Thank you for your letter of May 20, 2016 giving me the news of Wesley's home call into the Lord's presence on March 5, and also the worship order of service. My last communication from Wesley and yourself was the Christmas letter in December 2014.

You have had a long association with Wesley, firstly, I think, as his secretary, and then following Betty's passing, you had the joy and privilege of being married to him. I can understand how his severe stroke and sudden calling to glory must have been a tremendous shock to you.

While understandably Wesley's home call has left a vacuum in your life, what wonderful memories you must have of working with Wesley as his secretary, and then later for the seven years of marriage. Indeed I believe that you were God's gift to Wesley as his secretary—what hours you must have spent preparing his books for publication!! And also what a privilege! I want to assure you of our sympathy and our prayers at this time of loss. The words of an old paraphrase come to mind:

> *In every pang that rends the heart.*
> *The Man of Sorrows had a part;*
> *He sympathizes with our grief,*
> *And to the suff'rer sends relief.* (Based on Heb. 4:14ff)

I also share for your comfort, a very helpful passage from an obscure book in the Bible:

> *For the Lord will not cast off forever, but, though He cause grief, He will have compassion according to the abundance of his steadfast love (or mercy); For He does not willingly afflict or grieve the children of men.* (Lamentations 3:31-33, ESV)

Organizational and Individual Tributes

Joan and I went as missionaries to India with OMS 1964-1970. I first met Wesley in Northern Ireland in 1960. Wesley visited us in Madras in April 1967 (I think it was an OMS get-together). Then a year later there was another get-together in Allahabad (that was the only time we met Betty, Wesley's wife). We also met Wesley again when I was studying in Asbury Theological Seminary 1970-71 and also at the OMS Convention in Greenwood. We have always had the highest regard for Wesley and I have prayed for him for many years.

Finally, I note your assignment includes to help complete Wesley's autobiography. I had prayed that he would be able to complete it before he was called home to be with the Lord. When it is published, I would love to have a copy, if that will be possible. Thank you. May the Lord surround you with His love and peace.

With our love and prayers,
Norman and **Joan Duncan**, former OMS India missionaries, now pastor
Belfast, Northern Ireland, U.K.

He was a great inspiration to us and we so appreciated his prayers as well as his messages and books. He surely has been welcomed into heaven with the greeting 'Well done, thou good and faithful servant.'

David and **Marlys Fisher**, former OMS Board Member,
Prayer partners and supporters
Hubbard, IA

He impacted my life and is truly one of the great heroes of the faith and a great prayer warrior. We feel so blessed to have known him and got to hear him teach and read his books through the years.

Herb and **Ann Hornstra**, Prayer partners and supporters
Eugene, OR

Organizational and Individual Tributes

Wesley was reflecting God's glory, Christ's work on earth as he guided, prayed and encouraged John in some of his darkest hours.

John and **Karine McLaughlin,** MFM Cabinet and OMS Board member,
Prayer partners
Glidden, IA

Heaven now has rewards for such a faithful servant of our Lord and Christ. He was our backyard neighbor when we lived on Fairview Drive in Greenwood. We often visited and neighbored when he was home from OMS office. I have a beautiful lamp he carried on the plane in his lap when he came home from a trip to India.

Ray and **Eleanor Pottschmidt**, Prayer partners
Greenwood, IN

Wesley is rejoicing with his Lord and Savior. What a godly man! He was surely a willing servant.

Ward and **Dolly Rudy**, Prayer partners and supporters
Hedgesville, WV

Dr. Duewel was a very important part of our lives. We were honored to have him in our church several times and had him stay in our home once.

Cecile Truitt, wife of the late Dr. James Truitt, former OMS board member, Mother of Dr. Susan Truitt, OMS Korea missionary, Prayer partner and supporter
Woodway, TX

When we think of how Wesley has made a difference in this world, it is awesome! And not only that but how he lives on in our lives. A young friend and I are reading *'Ablaze for God'* together. I have a goal to read all his books.

Steve and **Jean Weber**, OMS volunteers
Greenwood, IN

Revival Prayer Fellowship

Please forgive us for being so slow in responding to your email of March, regarding the passing of Dr. Duewel. Barbara and I are so sorry to hear of his home going. He is now absent from his body and present with the Lord. May the Lord Jesus daily comfort you and the family, as you mourn your husband's and father's passing. You have our love, sympathy, and condolences. I'm so glad to hear that you will carry on his literature ministry. As I continue to promote his books, I will need to restock.

Last week, I shared at our Wednesday morning Ministers Prayer Gathering from Wesley's book *"Ablaze for God,"* page 29. This book is so moving and stirring, and focuses on the great spiritual needs among church leaders. God bless and comfort you.

In His Service,
LaRue Goetz, President
Revival Prayer Fellowship, Bismarck, ND

The Wesleyan Church

We are very saddened to hear of Dr. Duewel's passing. Many people are in Heaven because of his life's work. I attached this article from The Wesleyan Church's Online Magazine for you to read.

Our sympathies are with you and the family!
Rodger Kirkpatrick, Director of Operations
Wesleyan Church Headquarters, Fishers, IN

The Passing of Wesley Duewel

I received word recently that the great missionary saint, Dr. Wesley Duewel, passed away March 5, 2016, at the age of 99. His devotional classic, *"Ablaze for God"* is one of my favorites. I have read and re-read it many times, and it has been a tremendous source of spiritual strength and blessing to me. Seven years ago, our congregation was transformed as we went through this powerful book together. We invited Dr. Duewel, then age 92, to Hayward so he could share his heart and pray with us. To my delight, he accepted the invitation.

Obtaining special permission, I eagerly awaited Dr. Duewel's arrival at Gate A-19 of Minneapolis International Airport. His plane landed, and a long line of passengers debarked–but no Wesley Duewel. The last stragglers came out of the tunnel, but there was still no sign of my special guest. I checked with the agent who radioed back into the plane, and grunted, "*He's coming. He's coming*." Finally, three flight attendants emerged from the jet bridge, and they were all wiping away tears. One approached me, "*Are you the one waiting for that precious little old man back there*?" she blubbered. "*He was just praying for us! It was so beautiful! I have never felt such love in all my life*!"

I marveled. This holy man was so filled with God's presence and anointing that it automatically overflowed to everybody he met along the way. In other words, his very presence created a momentary place for others, where heaven and earth merged together. I lifted an eye towards heaven and prayed, "*Lord, when I grow up, please make me the kind of guy who makes flight attendants cry*!"

Mark O. Wilson, Senior Pastor
Hayward Wesleyan Church, Hayward, Wisconsin

Treasures in Christ

The Reality of Throne Life

Jesus promises, *"To the one who is victorious, I will give the right to sit with me on my throne, just as I was victorious and sat down with my Father on his throne"* (Rev. 3:21).

But that sitting is future, after we join Him in heaven, after the judgment seat of Christ, when He gives to us his rewards and honors. Even now Jesus wants you to exercise an active throne life. Christ has identified with us so fully that He provides for each true follower a gracious provision beyond our asking or thinking. It would be audacious and even blasphemous for you to suggest or claim the life that I now present if God's inspired Word did not clearly teach it.

Christ's provision for you is that by God's grace and your faith you can appropriate and experience to a sacred degree Christ's death, resurrection, and exaltation. You can know the reality of being crucified with Christ (Gal. 2:20), raised with Christ (Eph. 2:6), and now seated with Christ already on His throne.

God has already *"blessed us in the heavenly realms with every spiritual blessing in Christ"* (Eph. 1:3). We are members of the body, of which He is head, so what happened to Him happens spiritually to us. He is the Vine and we are the branches. We are in Him, and He in us. The language is figurative, but the words are to be taken as true spiritual reality.

Potentially, you are already exalted to the throne where He reigns actually. Although you are still here on earth, your spirit is in the heavenlies with Christ. You are in the world but not of it (John 17:11, 14). In spirit, you are lifted above the worldly, the earthly, and the temporal.[1]

Bishop Moule in his commentary on Ephesians 2:6 points out that because you are embodied *"in Christ,"* you are beside him on His throne of intercessory dominion. *"Believers are bodily in heaven in point of right, and virtually so in spirit, and have their own place assigned there, which in due time they shall take possession of."*[2]

You are spiritually to share Christ's exaltation now. You are to participate in a throne life and role now. You will possess in heaven visibly only what you possess now spiritually.

Since all things are under Christ's feet *(Eph. 1:22)* and you are *"in Christ,"* then all things are potentially under your feet also.

Paul assured the believers in Rome, *"The God of peace will soon crush Satan under your feet"* (Rom. 16:20). Is not this what Jesus referred to when He said, *"I have given you authority to trample on snakes and scorpions and to overcome all the power of the enemy"* (Luke 10:19)?

---

[1] ***Mighty Prevailing Prayer*** #34 You Must Prevail Over People (pp. 57-58)

[2] ***Commentary Practical and Explanatory on the Whole Bible*** *p. 1284*

This conquest must be accomplished through prevailing intercession. Then you realize the power to crush Satan. By faith, in virtue of Christ's cross and in His name, you can even issue commands to Satan. From your position where you are seated with Christ on the throne, you look down in spiritual vision upon Satan. In the words of Luther,

"And though this world, with devils filled,
Should threaten to undo us,
We will not fear, for God hath willed
His truth to triumph through us.
The Prince of Darkness grim,
We tremble not for him;
His rage we can endure,
For lo, his doom is sure;
One little word shall fell him."

"The life he lived, and the way in which he lived it, will continue to be a poignant spiritual challenge to us and many others. We are so grateful for the life and ministry of Dr. Wesley Duewel. We rejoice with you as his family and express deep gratitude to our Lord for a life extremely well lived for God's honor and glory."[3]

Father, after looking at what Dr. Wesley L. Duewel accomplished in his life of service to you and the kingdom, help us be more conscious in our own efforts to obey the calling on our lives. May the reality of his throne life influence us to accept the responsibility placed on us as Christians. The conquest of Satan's schemes must be accomplished through prevailing intercession. This I know! When we realize the power at our disposal because of what Christ has done on our behalf, may we put him

[3] Dr. Robert Fetherlin, President, One Mission Society

under our feet in situations that rise up. I ask this to Christ's glory, and in His name.

Amen,
Jean Oathoat, Internet blogger
Madrid, NY

Talitha Kumi International

My condolences on the sudden death of Dr. Wesley Duewel. He was really a man of God and I strongly believe, His soul is with the Almighty Lord and resting in peace. I arrived last Saturday to Dhaka, please convey my condolence to Mrs. Duewel.

Thank you and Blessings,
Philip Adhikary, Bishop
Talitha Kumi International, Dhaka, Bangladesh

Youth for Christ

Thanks so much for giving me this news. I knew Dr. Duewel and he had asked me to join him a few times at programs in India. I could never arrange that. He was a wonderful servant of God and a few of his books really impacted me. His book "*Touch the World through Prayer*" has been published in my language (Sinhala) and has had a very good impact.

I thank God for his influence,
Ajith Fernando, National Director
Youth for Christ, Sri Lanka

Death in Christ

For those in Christ death is a sleep.
The loving Shepherd leads His sheep
Into a pasture large and green,
More beautiful than man has seen.
And there, forever saved and blest,
They share with Christ His perfect rest.

For those in Christ death is a door;
He leads where He has gone before.
It opens on a fuller life,
Freed from all tension, fear, and strife.
It closes sorrow out and pain,
But opens to eternal gain.

For those in Christ death is a dawn,
With night and dark forever gone.
It ushers in a perfect day
With all fulfilled for which we pray—
A day of gladness, joy, and light,
Where God's own glory thrills man's sight.

For those in Christ death is a way
That leads from earth to heaven's day.
It leads to fellowship once more
With all in Christ who've gone before.
It leads to love, perfect and sweet,
In endless joy at Jesus' feet.

Wesley L. Duewel, October 22, 1958
Glasgow, Scotland

Gospel Message

Opening Prayer

Let us bow our heads and our hearts for prayer: *O Lord, Father of all mercies and God of all comfort; have compassion, we pray, upon all of us gathered here today, that our hearts and minds will be attuned to Your Spirit. Grant that this service of celebration and comfort, which we now hold in your name, may give all of us a sense of your gracious Presence and increase our trust and hope in you. May the peace of Christ that passes all understanding, reside with us and rest upon all these dear bereaved ones. We pray in the name of Jesus Christ, our Savior and Lord. Amen.*

Introduction:

It's been a great privilege to be a coworker of Dr. Wesley Duewel. He was the OMS President who sent our original acceptance letter in December of 1980. He was the OMS President who first challenged us with the "*Decade of Harvest*" vision from 1982–1992. He was the OMS President Emeritus who worked tirelessly for the cause of Christ through mighty prevailing prayer, fully surrendered preaching, and Spirit-anointed writing and publication. He was an inspiration and legendary hero of the mission who did everything possible to glorify and honor Christ Jesus and establish His Church around the world.

Due to the fact that he was in his 99th year and experiencing increased health issues, when we received the news from Hilda (through Dr. Fetherlin) that he had graduated to glory, we were not surprised, but we were deeply saddened. The passing of one who has enjoyed such long life, and has been a spiritual blessing to so many people, always brings sadness to those who loved and respected him so much. When Wesley and Hilda would leave the office, he would glance down the hall into my office and express his cheerful greeting: "*Blessings*." One day when they were leaving the office, I looked up to return my "*Have a good afternoon*" reply, but there was something about him that looked more frail and fragile than normal. The Lord seemed to speak to my spirit: "*He won't be with you much longer. I am calling him home soon.*" I always felt blessed just to have known him, so on that particular occasion I got up and walked with them to their vehicle, for what turned out to be, one of the final visits he made to his office.

Body:

In preparation for this day some years ago, Dr. Duewel wrote: "*A possible text for the speaker is Romans 1:15. In the King James Version it is, "As much as in me is, I am ready." The Living Bible gives it, "To the fullest extent of my ability, I am ready." Particularly, in my recent years that has been the desire of my heart to be ready for whatever God had for me*." Dr. Duewel was saying that he was ready to share the Gospel, to pray for evangelism, revival and missions, or to go to heaven. He was ready to do anything for anybody, and to go anywhere at any time, '*All for Jesus*.'

In Romans 1:8-17, esp. 15 Paul is saying, "*I am ready and willing. There's nothing that I'd rather do than to preach the Gospel in Rome, even though it's a world capital, no greater place of politeness and grandeur, a place where it might seem peculiarly dangerous to oppose those popular superstitions to which the empire is supposed to owe its greatness, happiness, and notoriety: yet still, in whatever circumstances, I am willing, no I am anxious, to come and proclaim this divine message among you, though it should be at the expense of my reputation, my liberty, or my life*."[1]

Paul dispelled any notion that he had been holding back from a trip to Rome due to any considerations or conjectures, like being ashamed to share the Gospel there. Having already affirmed the credentials of his Apostolic calling, he waived all privileges of rank and all the honors of such an office and presented himself in this verse to the total population of that great city, not merely as an ambassador, which he surely was, but also as a brother, a fellow Christian who loved them, prayed for them, and longed to visit them. Choosing exactly the right words, Paul in this perfect introduction, presented himself as one who actually considered himself in debt to the whole community, indeed to all people, and as a brother in Christ who was eager to share the Good News with them. How tender and beautiful are the sentiments expressed upon this sacred page! As one commentator put it:

> Our spirits are humbled before one who stood so high in the service of so great a Master. But now the Ambassador of Christ comes to us like one of ourselves. Across the waters which roll between him and us, we hear a brother's voice, and see a brother's face.[2]

Likewise, Dr. Wesley Duewel was a tremendous man of so many outstanding, unequaled, spiritual characteristics. These verses speak very descriptively and are equally appropriate when applied to this giant of a man today. The tributes we've heard today are emblematic of the vast numbers that could be shared, if those people whom Dr. Duewel touched around the world were able to be present with us.

---

[1] Coke's Commentary on the Whole Bible

[2] Coffman's Commentaries on the Bible

At the same time, Dr. Duewel was first and foremost a husband, father, grandfather, great grandfather, and fellow believer who loved you, prayed for you, and longed to be with you. He considered himself in debt to his family, his friends, and the whole world, to all people, eager to share the Good News of Jesus with anyone and everyone.

1. The Apostle Paul said, *"I thank my God for all of you. God is my witness how constantly I remember you in my prayers at all times. I long to see you that you and I may be mutually encouraged by each other's faith"* (Rom. 1:8-11).

During these latter years of your father's and grandfather's life, while we served together in the Research and Writing Center, I would occasionally stop in to chat with him, and try to imbibe the great burden and passion of his heart. If I had any heavy burden or concern, I would take it to him and he would be happy to intercede on my behalf. He had such a close personal relationship with Jesus that I knew if anyone was going to get through to God, he could. He spoke to God in prayer like He was his best friend, and indeed He was.

But before we concluded our conversations, it was common for him to ask me to remember the concerns and cares that he carried for his family. He was a father of grateful, thoughtful, and heartfelt prayer. He would pray, thanking God for all of you. He would pray, constantly remembering you in his prayers at all times. We would join our hearts in prayer for you, John, Christine, and Darlene and your families. Your father and grandfather carried a greater burden than he ever showed in public. The gratefulness and burden of his heart was laid bare in prayer. He would pray choking back tears, and when he couldn't compose himself anymore, I witnessed tears streaming down his cheeks for you, his children and family. Like Paul, your father and grandfather longed to see you so that he might have imparted to you some spiritual gift to make you stronger, and ultimately so that you and he would have been mutually encouraged by each other's faith. Like Paul, he prayed that by some means, a way would be opened for you to come to the fullness of the glorious Gospel that carried and sustained him throughout his life.

2. The Apostle Paul said, "*I am obligated and eager to preach the Gospel*" (Rom. 1:14-15). Your father, grandfather, and friend, was always ready and urgently burdened to share the Good News of salvation in Jesus Christ. He left instructions for me to not spend too much time talking about him personally. He said, "*Talk about my wonderful Savior, whose I am, and whom I sought to serve. Talk about His grace to me*." He would pray that '*the earth would be filled with the knowledge of the glory of the LORD as the waters cover the sea,*' because he felt himself obligated and eager to preach the Good News of salvation in Jesus Christ.

3. The Apostle Paul also said, "*For I am not ashamed of the Gospel, because it is the power of God that brings salvation to everyone who believes …. For in the Gospel the righteousness of God is revealed — a righteousness that is by faith from first to last, just as it is written*: "*The righteous will live by faith*" (Rom. 1:16-17). Your father, grandfather, and fellow believer, loved the Lord with all of his heart, and was not embarrassed, or hesitant, to encourage others to do the same. He was '*always ready to share the reason for the hope that was within him in tenderness and humility,*' for he was not ashamed of the Gospel of Jesus Christ.

The Gospel of Jesus Christ is glorious Good News. '*Glory*' is a very important word. When it comes to Jesus no other word will do. The glory of something is its weight, its unique worth. It's what sets something apart in a unique way. The glory of a sunset is its color; the glory of a lion is its strength; the glory of a master craftsman is his skill. In Jesus we see the glory of the character and presence of the Triune God.

God's glory is too much to comprehend. When Peter, James, and John caught a glimpse of it as Jesus was transfigured in blazing brilliance on the mountain top, Peter stuttered and stammered because he was so overwhelmed (Mk. 9:6). On the island of Patmos, John the Beloved saw the risen Jesus in all His glory and *"he fell down at His feet as though dead"* (Rev. 1:17). This is the glory of God seen in Jesus: and Jesus Himself said it was reflected most clearly of all, not on the mountain top, not on the island of Patmos, but on the Cross of Calvary (John 12:23-24).

What should our response be to this glory? *"At the name of Jesus every knee should bow and every tongue confess that Jesus Christ is Lord to the glory of God the Father"* (Rom. 14:11). Jesus Himself tells us how He should be treated. He expects us, motivated by love, to obey him. As its creator, He has authority over the world He has made. He speaks to His disciples then and now: *"<u>All</u> authority in heaven and earth is given to me. Therefore, go and make disciples of <u>all</u> nations. Teaching them to obey <u>all</u> that I have commanded you. And remember, I am with you at <u>all</u> times."* (Mt. 28:18-20). The four '*<u>alls</u>*' are quite comprehensive in their breadth and application:

<u>All</u> authority in heaven and earth has been given to me. (There is no authority, but His authority, His Power, and His might!)
Go, therefore, and make disciples of <u>all</u> nations . . . . (Every tongue and tribe, all ethnic groups, all peoples on this earth)
Teaching them to obey <u>all</u> that I have commanded you, (The whole council of God, every jot and iota of the precious Word of God.)

Gospel Message

Remember, I am with you at <u>all</u> times. (He will never, ever leave us or forsake us.)

The glory of Jesus is not just in His presence, power and authority, supreme as those are. To glorify His name is to be overwhelmed by the significance, the sweetness of His sacrifice. He *"came to them"* in Mt. 28:18, after He had risen from the dead, with the nail marks in His hands and feet, and the spear mark in His side, still fresh in His skin. Now He sits on the Throne of Heaven as the crucified and resurrected one, as Rev. 5:5-6 puts it, as *"a Lamb, looking as if it had been slain*." At this point it gets very, very personal because every believer knows that Jesus the Lamb of God was slain for each one of us:

He was pierced for our transgressions,
He was crushed for our iniquities;
The punishment that was on Him brought us peace,
And by His wounds we are healed [or saved] (Is. 53:5).

He lived and walked and talked and led a band of followers. He was unjustly tried in a Roman and Jewish court. He was unfairly sentenced to death. He was beaten, smitten, flogged within an inch of his life; forced to carry his own instrument of death. He was strung up on that cruel Roman Cross; a makeshift crown of thorns shoved down on His brow; a spear thrust through His side. He was taken down from the Cross and declared fully and completely dead.

Jesus went down into the valley of the shadow of death where criminals die. He carried our sin, our shame, our rebellion, our failures, in his own, broken and bruised, crushed and crucified incarnate body. He heaps all our garbage on his back and climbs onto the Cross, where He was punished for our crimes, and died a bloody, gruesome death that should have been ours. The innocent God-Man is punished for the guilty.

Three days later He was seen walking around again! The resurrection of Jesus Christ proves to us that there is life beyond death, life after the tomb, and Jesus is in charge of it! Its past certainty gives us a future hope. It means that no matter how much death appears to have won, nor how defeated we may feel today, we can still walk in victory. Can you see what the One with all authority has done for us? Can you see how much He loved us? For those who abused, mocked, ridiculed, and rejected Him, He stretched out His arms and died for us? He loved us this much!

The Gospel of Jesus Christ is the good and true account that Jesus has defeated evil, sin, shame, and death through His own death and resurrection, and is making all things new, even us.

Today there is no escaping discussions about choices. Rejecting Jesus has infinite consequences (Lk. 10:16). But Jesus is the way. For those who embrace Jesus in His sin-absorbing, shame-dissolving death, there is forgiveness, restoration, and new life. He deals justly with our crimes by taking our place as our substitute. Jesus pleads our innocence before the Father, and His redemption restores our relationship with God. Realizing this should make us incredibly grateful and humble. The Good News of salvation in Jesus Christ reveals how underserving we are, and it shows us just how much mercy we have been given.

Today there is no escaping discussions about truth. All other religions teach that human beings must work their way toward divinity (John 14:6). But Jesus is the truth. The truth is not found in our attempts to climb a spiritual ladder to God, to experience a vision of the divine. He is

Gospel Message

God coming down to us, becoming one of us, dying in our place, for our crimes. God comes to us, delivering us from our well-deserved spiritual death, and in exchange, giving us His abundant and eternal life. The Good News of salvation in Jesus Christ reveals how God comes down to humanity – that's pure divine grace!

Today there is no escaping discussions about life and death. In John the Beloved's Gospel, Jesus says that He is the resurrection and the life, that whoever believes in Him though they die physically, yet they shall live spiritually (John 11:25). But Jesus is the life. He descends into the valley to take our death, rising up from the dead, and ascending to prepare a new place for us to enjoy everlasting life with Him forever. In the end, it doesn't matter how nice and moral a person is, because there is not enough niceness or morality to pay for our rejection of God's great grace. Either we are rejected, or we turn to Jesus who was rejected for us. This is the heart of the Gospel. Jesus lay down His life for those who reject Him, for His enemies, for those who don't believe Him, and He offers them forgiveness.

The Gospel is the good and true account of the defeat of death, the overthrow of evil through the self-sacrifice of the only sinless and blameless person who ever lived, the God-man, Christ Jesus.

The Gospel of Jesus Christ is Good News whether someone perceives it to be or not. Those who have placed their trust in Jesus know it is good because they experience its grace-saturated goodness in their everyday lives. We know the Gospel is good, not just in theory, but because the reality of its grace permeates our experiences of parenting, playing, praying, working, suffering, and every other human experience. We know the Gospel is good because it frees us from others' opinions, when, through faith in Christ, we have the only opinion that really matters, God the Father, who says through the witness of His Spirit: "*You are my children with whom I am well pleased*." This deep undying love and approval of God the Father frees us from people-pleasing, over-working, spouse-impressing, self-adoring living. We can live free from the influence of others. We can live free from the opinions of others. We can live free from the condemnation of others. We can live in the liberty of the certainty of tomorrow. Jesus has liberated us from the guilt and shame of yesterday, the enslavements and bondage of today, and He has our future all wrapped up.

The only response to the One with all power being crucified in our place is to echo the words: "*Glory, Glory, Glory, all power and glory be yours, sweet Jesus*." We should carry with us an overwhelming sense of gratitude and worship. Our present and our future is guaranteed by the resurrection of Jesus. He says: "*I am the Living One; I was dead, and now look, I am alive for ever more! And I hold the keys of death and Hell*" (Rev. 1:18)!

The exciting truth is, now, today, anyone can enjoy a personal, vital, vibrant, relationship with Jesus. In Rev. 21:6 Jesus compares this intimacy with life giving, life enhancing, life fulfilling, 'living water' when He says, "*To the thirsty I will give water without cost from the spring of the water of life*." Who doesn't thirst for this 'living water' of life? Everyone is striving for this quality of life; this level of intimacy with God. The problem is, most people look for this 'water' in all the wrong places. It's only offered and available in Jesus, as He told the woman at the well who had made a mess of her life by looking in the wrong places: "*Whoever drinks the water I give them will never thirst. Indeed the water I give them will become in them a spring of water welling up to eternal life*" (John 4:14). Jesus came to give 'living water' at no cost to those who accept it, but at a monumental cost to Himself. He came to ensure that we have a better, richer, fuller life now, and on into eternity, beyond what we can ever imagine.

Closing:

Here are some key questions that Dr. Duewel would like us to consider: Are you certain about your relationship with God the Father through Jesus Christ? Are you excited about the intimacy available to you in Jesus Christ through the Holy Spirit? In your heart and mind is your relationship with the Triune God assured? If it isn't, this is a great opportunity to ensure that future by placing your trust in the redemptive work of Jesus Christ today.

Your father, grandfather, and friend followed faithfully a three-fold passion: He was passionate for evangelism, revival, and mission harvest. He was not involved in missions for the sake of mission activity, not merely for staying busy for 'busy-ness' sake. He was passionate about earnest prayer, the foundation for all other ministries, with the result that there would be a harvest even in seemingly unresponsive areas of the world, like India. He said: *"I fear most missionary work is not covered by enough prayer. It takes prayer to give souls. This is why I have pled for earnest, committed prayer. This is why I believe in and have used prayer lists, time in prayer, and endeavored to develop solid prayer habits."* Prayer affords everyone here today, the opportunity to act upon the lasting desire and personal passion of Dr. Wesley Duewel, to invite the life-giving Spirit of God into every willing person's life.

Shall we pray?

Dear Lord, send the seal of your Presence upon every heart in this service this day by the witness of your Spirit. We ask you to heal the broken hearted and bind up their wounds; mercifully look upon those who are bereaved. Be near them in their sorrow, and let it draw them nearer unto you. Earthly joys and comforts fail. But your grace sustains and strengthens. May the things unseen and eternal grow more real, more present, filled with increasing meaning and power in all of our lives. May your Spirit bear witness with every person's spirit, inviting, encouraging, and consoling. Let your strength sustain our weakness; and your peace fill our hearts and minds with perfect trust in you. Comfort the distraught, assure the grateful, and abide with all of us until we too hear Thy precious voice welcoming us home. In Jesus' name we pray. Amen.

David E. **Dick**, VP At Large
One Mission Society, Greenwood, IN

Gospel Message

Prayer Introduction to Solo

Dr. Duewel wrote: *"I have loved and prayed for my family members and loved ones for years. I want us all to love Jesus, serve Him here on earth, and be a blessing to others. I want to spend the endless years of eternity with all of you in heaven. I chose this song for any of my dear ones who may have thus far failed to make their clear-cut, total commitment to Jesus. Please don't delay–the longer you delay, the more rewards that Jesus longs to give you will be missed by your delay. I love you. I want to spend eternity with you. I want to rejoice eternally over your abundant eternal reward. Please accept this song with love. – Wesley."*

I Dreamed I Searched Heaven for You

I dreamed I had gone to that city,
That city where never comes night,
And I saw the bright angels in glory,
I saw the fair mansions of light;
I gazed for long, long years of rapture,
On the face of my Savior so true,
And I sang with the seraphim holy,--
Then I dreamed I searched heaven for you.

Chorus:
I dreamed I searched heaven for you,
Searched vainly thru heaven for you;
Friend, won't you prepare to meet me up there?
Lest we should search heaven for you.

Gospel Message

I looked on both sides of the river,
That flows thro' the city of God,
I searched thro' bright mansions celestial,
And streets of gold pavement I trod;
The faces of saints by the million,
I scanned in my yearning to see
That face I had cherished so fondly,--
The face that had grown dear to me.

I asked of ten thousand sweet angels,
"Have you seen this belov'd one? Pray tell,
Have you met in the bright courts of heaven
That one whom on earth we loved well?
They shook their heads sadly and told me
That they had not seen you,
And then I knew that some-
where in the darkness,
You wandered, lost, lost in sin.

James D. Vaughan, © 1932
Lawrenceburg, TN

EFMA Lifetime Service Award, Dallas, TX – September 2007

Wesley and Hilda's Wedding Day December 27, 2008
Witnessed by OMS President Dr. and Mrs. David Long

Conclusion

Are You Hiding the Word of God?

One Christmas season, about 25 miles distant from Allahabad Bible Seminary (ABS), on the final night of the practical ministry assignment, Dr. Duewel, some students, and the villagers were sitting around a camp fire on the ground under the open sky and the bright stars overhead. After singing several Gospel songs in their language, Wesley picked up a rather large Hindi Bible and began to read them the beautiful Christmas story from Luke chapter two.

Among the villagers sitting on the ground cross-legged was an old, white-haired, bare-chested man, who interrupted and asked: "*How many years is it since God's Son was born*?" Wesley endeavored to assist the man with his own answer by asking another question. "*Can you read*?" Asked Dr. Duewel: "*Have you ever received a letter in the mail? What was the number the government puts on the outside of the letter? Or if you have gone to the court house, what is the number they put on your papers*?"

The villagers talked among themselves for a minute or two, "*1943*," they replied. Wesley replied: "*That's right," it is about that many years since the Great Day that God's Son was born nearly 2,000 years ago*."

"*2,000 years*!" he exclaimed. Then pointing his finger at Wesley, he asked: "*Who has been hiding that book all this time? Why have you never told us before*?" Dr. Duewel answered: "*Well, I don't think anyone has been trying to hide it. You see, the world is a big world and tonight we have come to your village to tell you*."

Conclusion

That seemed to satisfy the man and the other villagers, but that night Wesley returned to his tent with that question turning over and over in his mind. He could not sleep. He kept hearing that man's question. "*Who's been hiding that book all this time*?" Ten o'clock became midnight, and finally at two o'clock in the morning he got out his flashlight, paper and pen, and wrote these words:

Are you hiding the Word of God?

You have the words which the Savior gave,
You have the book which millions crave,
You have the truth which alone can save –
Are you hiding the Word of God?

Millions are groping in sin's dark night,
Searching the pathway to truth and right.
You in your hands have the only light –
Are you hiding the Light of God?

Millions engage in a deadly strife,
Foes of the soul and God are rife;
Millions are losing the fight for life –
Are you hiding the Sword of God?

The need still exists though seasons roll,
Millions are fainting far short their goal,
Millions tonight have a hungry soul –
Are you hiding the Bread of God?

Conclusion

Millions haste on to a Christ-less tomb,
Treading the pathways of sin and gloom,
You, if you will, can avert their doom –
Will you give them the Word of God?

Wesley L. Duewel, Circa 1943
Allahabad, Uttar Pradesh, India

Well-Known and Beloved Mission Leader Dies

Dr. Wesley L. Duewel, 99, passed away on March 5, 2016. Born on June 3, 1916, in St. Charles, Missouri, to the late Louis and Ida Luelf Duewel, Dr. Duewel heard God's call to India at the age of five in Nashville, Illinois. He gave his heart and soul for the cause of Christ and world missions for the past 75 years, where he served faithfully with One Mission Society (OMS).

Following ministry in India for nearly 25 years, Dr. Duewel served as President of OMS from 1969-1982. Most recently, he served as President Emeritus and special assistant to the President for evangelism and intercession and was also working on his autobiography.

From early childhood, Dr. Duewel had a deep love for the Word of God. His writings and poems on the Holy Spirit, revival, and soul winning call God's people back to prayer, the source of all power for ministry and express his hunger and passion. More than 2.5 million copies of his 10 books are now in circulation in 58 languages worldwide.

Conclusion

Recognized as an authority on missions, Dr. Duewel served for 16 years on the board of directors of *Missio Nexus* (formerly the Evangelical Fellowship of Mission Agencies), as president from 1969-1972, 19 years on the North American Board of World Evangelical Fellowship, 20 years on the board of National Association of Evangelicals, and a life trustee of Asbury Theological Seminary. In 2007, *Missio Nexus* honored Dr. Duewel with their first-ever *Lifetime of Service Award*. In 2009, the *Evangelical Fellowship of India* presented him with the *Lifetime Service Award* in recognition of his servant leadership.

Dr. Duewel held the degrees of Doctor of Education from the University of Cincinnati and the Doctor of Divinity from Taylor University. His articles appeared in many publications, and for 12 years he edited *Revival Magazine*, published in 12 languages. He traveled widely ministering in 45 countries of the world.

He was a member of the Wabash Conference of the Free Methodist Church for 48 years. For years, Dr. Duewel taught a senior adult Sunday School class. He enjoyed sharing his testimony to God's faithfulness, with a deep concern for un-evangelized millions and a constant emphasis upon prayer as key to harvest and revival.

Dr. Duewel was preceded in death by his wife of 68 years, Elizabeth (Betty) Dolly Raisch, and is survived by a son, John Wesley (Retno), two daughters, Christine Zahniser (Ed) and Darlene Rueger (Terry); six grandchildren and three great-grandchildren; and current wife of seven years, Hilda Mae (Johnecheck) Duewel, also an OMS missionary.

Dr. Wesley and Mrs. Hilda Duewel

Darlene, Christine, Wesley, and John Duewel

The Duewels, Zahnisers, and Ruegers

Duewel Literature Trust Books

Ablaze for God
Zondervan Publishing, Grand Rapids. 1989. ($12 – 327 pages)

God's Great Salvation
Duewel Literature Trust, Greenwood, IN. 1991. ($10 – 332 pages)

God's Power is for You: *Reflections on the Deeper Life*
Zondervan Publishing, Grand Rapids. 1997. ($9 – 175 pages)

Heroes of the Holy Life: *Biographies of Fully Devoted Followers of Christ*, Zondervan Publishing, Grand Rapids. 2002. ($11 – 206 pages)

Let God Guide You Daily
Duewel Literature Trust, Greenwood, IN. 1988. ($9 – 224 pages)

Measure Your Life: *17 Ways to Evaluate Your Life from God's Perspective*, Duewel Literature Trust, Greenwood, IN. 1992. ($9 – 224 pages)

Mighty Prevailing Prayer: *Experiencing the Power of Answered Prayer*, Zondervan Publishing, Grand Rapids. 1990. ($12 – 336 pages)

More God, More Power: *Filled and Transformed by the Holy Spirit*
Zondervan Publishing, Grand Rapids. 2000. ($9 – 143 pages)

Revival Fire
Zondervan Publishing, Grand Rapids. 1995. ($12 – 384 pages)

Touch the World through Prayer
Zondervan Publishing, Grand Rapids. 1986. ($11 – 256 pages)

Wesley Duewel Internet Links

2007 Lifetime of Service Award video –
https://www.youtube.com/watch?v=3FLLE40Z3eo

Come to the Fire –
http://www.cometothefire.org/alethasjournal/?offset=1458907187538

Wesley Duewel Memorial Fund –
https://onemissionsociety.org/give/dr-wesley-duewel-memorial-fund

Wesley Duewel Memorial Service –
https://www.youtube.com/watch?v=LtjCNcCkYnk&feature=youtu.be

The Wesleyan Church –
https://www.wesleyan.org/4833/the-passing-of-wesley-duewel

Conclusion

Treasures in Christ –
http://jean-oathout.blogspot.com/2016_03_01_archive.html

Wesley Duewel Sermon Video Links

Dynamic Holy Hunger –
https://www.youtube.com/watch?v=8ZB3GutmMOM

Holy Hunger and Deeper Reigning with Christ –
https://www.youtube.com/watch?v=2pIlQOkoVYo

Heart-Cry for World-Wide Revival –
https://www.youtube.com/watch?v=WVG3zqS5JRc

Rend the Heavens and Come Down –
https://www.youtube.com/watch?v=Cns8k9DFPlI

Prayer is Asking –
https://www.youtube.com/watch?v=HaAWdsf0eAU

Prayer is Knocking –
https://www.youtube.com/watch?v=92mu_v6FDL8

Prayer is Seeking –
https://www.youtube.com/watch?v=JPaeQO80q9Q

Prevailing in Intercession (Part One) –
https://www.youtube.com/watch?v=eRFPJ7R6WNI

Conclusion

Prevailing in Intercession (Part Two) – https://www.youtube.com/watch?v=hO8iJpHiM8g

---

Index

Endicott	Scott	Page 103	CLC Publications
Erny	Edward	Page 88	OMS Retiree
Erny	Robert	Page 95	OMS Retiree
Esler	Ted	Page 116	Mission Nexus
Fernando	Ajith	Page 128	Youth for Christ
Fetherlin	Robert	Pages vii & 74	OMS President
Fisher	David	Page 121	Prayer Partner
Fisher	Marlys	Page 121	Prayer Partner
Gaul	Santi	Page 39	Granddaughter
Goetz	LaRue	Page 123	Revival Prayer Fellowship
Hardig	Warren	Page 82	Men For Missions Int'l
Harris	John	Page 60	Evangelical Ch of India
Hartadi	Firman	Page 68	Nusantara Evangelical Ch
Hess	Bruce	Page 95	OMS Retiree
Hess	Donna	Page 95	OMS Retiree
Hinthorn	Aletha	Page 53	Cousin and Author
Hornstra	Herb	Page 121	Prayer Partner
Hornstra	Ann	Page 121	Prayer Partner
Howell	William	Page 1	***For All The Saints***
Inoue	Takanori	Page 115	Japan Holiness Ch
Jacob	Wilma	Page 96	OMS Retiree
Jayakumar	Samuel	Page 60	Evangelical Ch of India
Kirkpatrick	Rodger	Page 124	Wesleyan Ch
Kolapudi	Cephas JohnHyde	Page 119	Operation Mobilization
Kruse	Roger	Page 80	OMS India
Kruse	Glenda	Page 80	OMS India
Loobie	Susan	Pages 158 & 159	OMS Comm.
Magee	Christine	Page 86	OMS Adult MK
Mangalraj	Isaac	Page 61	Evangelical Ch of India
Martinez	Juan	Page 111	Hagnos Publishing
Maxey	Gary	Page 117	WATS & New Beginning Ch
Maxey	Emma Lou	Page 117	WATS & New Beginning Ch

Conclusion

Conclusion